Unless otherwise noted, all scriptures taken
from

THE HOLY BIBLE, KING JAMES VERSION.
Public domain.

Editor: Karla Dial

Cover Design:

Kandra McBrattin (www.Deodigital.biz)

FIRST EDITION

www.billeelliotauthor.com

Endorsements

The Everlasting Gospel of Christ by Brian Christian is a truly amazing book. If you are hungry to know more about your true identity from an eternal perspective, then this book is filled with information that will do just that. I have known Apostle Brian for some time now and have enjoyed him being a guest on several of my Webinar broadcasts. What a privilege to be connected to this author and to interact with someone who pushes my theological buttons every time we talk. The Everlasting Gospel of Christ is a revelation of the Eternal Christ who lives within all creation. He is the eternal One who "is" always with us in oneness and union, and who "was" from the beginning of time, and who is to "come" or is manifesting each and every moment of our lives so that we know the revelation of the Father's mind. I definitely recommend this book for all readers.

Bishop Dr. Bill Hanshew, D.B.S., D.Th
World Bible School University,
Founder/Chancellor

Contents

Introduction

In today's twenty-first-century understanding of spirituality, there has been a tug of war between religions and Christian denominations. Everyone is trying to prove who is right and who is wrong. With doctrinal disputes and dogmatic declarations, our generation has struggled to see one another from a place of love and vulnerability. We strive to attain and when we fall short, we spiral into a mess of emotion that either leads us to condemn ourselves or others. If you have found yourself wandering through the wilderness of your own perceptions, feeling defeated and isolated, then this book is for you.

Why did God allow this to happen to me? Why didn't God deliver me when I cried out to Him? These are big questions with very few answers. And the answers we do hear only promote more striving, blame, and competition in and through the relationships around us.

But what if you could take a look into the mind of Jesus and catch a glimpse of His perspective? What if the way we have been taught the good-news Gospel has not really been from the Father's perspective of who you are?

I wrote this book because I have walked through a lot of this. Feeling like I was on the outside looking in, labeled as the black sheep, the outcast. So I would perform even harder, proving I was better than what I secretly believed.

I dealt with rejection from my family my entire childhood and into my adult life. When I was born again, I was rejected by the church and thrown away. This led to suicidal thoughts, depression, and the need to constantly protect myself. I clung to doctrines that would justify self-preservation and feed my ego, giving me a sense of purpose. But I was always waiting for the other shoe to drop.

Don't hope too much because it will probably be stolen from you again. And it was all because I was a disappointment to God.

Or so I believed.

If you can relate to my journey, then this book is for you! It was a long road of contradictions that would bring forth keys of freedom for my life and for many others. I'd like those keys to unlock doors for you too.

We are about to embark on a journey together that is going to deconstruct many perceptions you have about others, and even God. But once the veils are removed, you are going to meet yourself in God and others in ways you never thought possible.

If I were to ask, "What is your biggest struggle?" how would you answer the question? Most would point to circumstances or relationships in their lives. They would look at outward things as their problem. But what I have realized is the biggest problem is not what is going on around us but what *isn't* going on *within* us—not properly understanding the purpose of our present situations. To know the intentions of God in our circumstances would create a peace that would silence our need to figure things out. We could simply rest in the Father's embrace and walk like Jesus walked.

Jesus made a profound statement. He said, "I only do what I see the Father doing," and then He said, it was the Father doing the works through Him (**John 5:19, 14:10**). What if I told you that these two statements, when applied, would remove all the striving and spiritual gymnastics we as believers find ourselves entangled in? This is the heart of The Everlasting Gospel of Christ!

My wife and I have been traveling around the nation ministering these truths that we have now lived out for many years together. We have seen entire family lines transformed in six days through this revelation. Couples who could not see each other's hearts anymore became completely unified and fell in love all over again when they encountered these truths. Condemnation simply fell off them as they realized nothing in their lives was in vain but had a higher purpose; it was leading them somewhere else. Everywhere we have taught these principles, love and unity has been the fruit.

This is not because of a new doctrine or teaching, but a manifestation of truth through divine encounters. The last twenty-five years of trial and error has now become this book to aid others in the posture of true identity as sons and daughters of God.

Before you start reading, I want you to understand the posture of encountering what is written in these pages. I believe what I walked through in life, which I once called trauma, is now the platform for glory! I wasn't just walking in my own shoes, but in the shoes of many in order to create a bridge of relatability and expression that would highlight the goodness and grace of our heavenly Father in and through you.

We are going to travel many trails together in the pages ahead, and some might feel dangerous. Some things might seem too deep to comprehend with your own understanding, and that is by design; it is the nature of encounter. How we have depended upon human reasoning and logic must be targeted and brought subject to divine encounters of truth.

I promise you this: if you will simply drink and try not to think, what you cannot comprehend will circle around to apprehend you. Many have testified to this truth. They told me it went over their head, but then it came back and hovered and all of a sudden it was like a memory of truth invading their lives. Identity was activated, and they found themselves simply partnering with the Spirit.

They were watching the Father do the works.

But before we can partner, we have to allow revelation to obliterate our need to figure things out. Oh, how the ego needs to understand in order to be in control! But you will have to leave conclusions at the door before entering this book. What conclusions you do bring in will be confronted and adjusted.

This is a book for the mystic, the intellectual, the scientist, and the philosopher. You might not get everything written in this book, but you will get what the Father is currently emphasizing in your life. The Everlasting Gospel of Christ is about the journey of all humanity before time began—what motivated us to come to Planet Earth, the reason we chose spiritual amnesia, and the unconditional love demonstrated through our weaknesses and failures. We will time-travel together into the very memories of the testimony of God and watch the scriptures open them to us. We will see previous truths we have known go to another level, taking us from *doing* the will of God to being His will. Your history of trauma will become your greatest asset as the Father reveals His intentions in your journey. Everything will become profitable as you witness God exceeding what you can imagine. Your warfare will cease as you enter the rest of God.

So get ready to meet yourself before time began and then watch the convergence of who you were move into who you are. Don't think, just drink! If you don't understand, then stand under. For it is time to unlearn what has been learned that you might learn to yearn for a face-to-face embrace of Father's grace.

Brian Christian

July 2020

Chapter One

Eternity and Chaos

To the weak became I as weak, that I might gain the weak: I am made all things to all men, that I might by all means save some (1 Corinthians 9:22)

Before we dig into mysteries and chew on the meat of revelation, I want to share my journey of divinely orchestrated personal chaos. This is what catapulted me into the eternal realm of bliss and transformed my life. It is amazing how love can change past weakness and loss, impacting the lives of many for good.

I have been forerunning this revelation that I call "The Everlasting Gospel" since 2002. But I did not see the fruit I anticipated for many years.

I had a lot of issues in my spiritual walk from the beginning of my awakening in 1986. I was the first in my family to experience redemption; everyone else was still chasing their tales. I was a loner, so I was on my own for many years. I came from a family that did not really know how to love, and my father was out of the picture by the time I was five years old, which made me want to prove myself even more. My testimony of grace is quite amazing, but the road was long and hard.

My dad tried to kill me while I was still in my mother's womb. He kicked my mother several times in the stomach with steel-toed boots to get rid of me. My family used to use the term "the good old days before Brian was born." They believed I was an accident and should never have been born. They had no clue this would affect me for many years to come.

My stepdad came on the scene when I was six years old. He introduced me to marijuana within a few months of moving in. On my birthday, I received a subscription to *Playboy* magazine and began my journey into porn addiction and objectifying women. Every Christmas, Santa Claus would leave marijuana, magic mushrooms, and LSD in my stocking.

I was left to my own devices and became a very angry little boy. By the time I was twelve years old, I was trying to run the house as well as deal drugs to the neighborhood kids. I had dabbled in witchcraft and satanism and had a really strong curiosity about the supernatural. I remember chasing my two younger half-brothers around with a drill, threatening to kill them before my mom told me to stop. My response was to threaten her as well.

But when I did put down the drill, I headed to the kitchen table to play with my Ouija board. With my hand hovering over the planchette which moves over the board to spell out words, it began to move of its own accord. Slowly, it spelled: R-E-P-E-N-T. I had no idea what that meant and was about to get up when a mist of water hit me from above. It was like someone took a squirt bottle and misted it above me. There was no one around me when it happened.

But what came next was even more amazing.

Immediately, I could not move. Waves and waves of love began pouring over me, and I began to weep. I had no understanding at the time that it was God, but I knew I was sorry for every evil thing I had done.

The Ouija board than spelled out the words, "Go and I will be with you." It spelled out a date, a time, and a place I was to go to that week. Thinking this was my spirit guide, I obeyed and went.

It was late summer of 1986 and I had turned sixteen just a few months earlier. I found myself at the address I had been given; it was a church. I had no clue what church was or how it was supposed to be. I didn't realize for many years that the church I went to that day was completely dead. In fact, two weeks after I attended that one church service, the pastor divorced his wife, quit the ministry, and left to become an Elvis Presley impersonator. How's that for crazy?

But the day the Ouija board told me to go was life-changing. I sat in a pew about ten rows back on the right side of the church. I could feel every eye on me and felt they knew everything about me. I couldn't hide anything that had happened to me. As the pastor got up to preach, all his words got twisted up and it was like a foreign language. Something had scrambled my hearing and it sounded like the way adults spoke in the *Charlie Brown* cartoons.

Then all of a sudden, everything went white. There was total silence; I was no longer in the church. I saw a huge pair of hands come out of this pure light, and they had holes in them.

In a flash, everything returned to normal and the pastor made an altar call. Without thought or understanding, I ran to the front of the church. The leaders took me into a back room with a few other kids and we held hands in a circle. I was told to repeat a prayer, which later I would come to know as "the sinner's prayer." I still had no clue that I was now born again. I had not heard the Gospel with natural ears; I simply encountered it, with no understanding.

I left that day with no burdens upon me. With ear-to-ear smiles, I walked back toward my house. It would take five books to tell you everything that happened over the next few years, but I will tell you this:

I tried going back to my sex, drugs, and rock and roll lifestyle, but couldn't. I was actually on the verge of suicide because I couldn't enjoy the life I had before. I thought something was wrong with me because I just couldn't bring myself to live the way I used to.

From the first day of my conversion, I began encountering angels and realms of heaven. I thought it was flashbacks from all the drugs I had done, so I just wrote it off as being in my mind.

But within a year, the Lord began to tell me that I was called to change a generation. Now, you have to understand this was the 1980s. I had attended an Assemblies of God church, so at least they believed in being filled with the Spirit and moving in the gifts. But though they believed *doctrinally*, they never actually *moved* in it. Prophetic ministry in those days would be a general prophetic word spoken in King James language over the congregation. Personal prophecy was considered fortune-telling and was forbidden.

But God spoke to me and gave me two scriptures:

Before I formed thee in the belly I knew thee; and before thou camest forth out of the womb I sanctified thee, and I ordained thee a prophet unto the nations (Jeremiah 1:5).

and

For I will shew him how great things he must suffer for my name's sake (Acts 9:16).

I had no clue what I was about to walk through, nor did I understand the concept of being chosen before I was born. All was hidden from me for many years as to the purpose of the Father in and through my life.

The Lord also told me, "You will be a father to many, you will be an example as a husband, and your marriage will restore many marriages." He also said, "You will be a unifier to the Body of Christ."

What was my response? Being the extremist I was, I left everything and started preaching on the streets. I was seventeen years old when I began my ministry.

People ask me now, "How did you just leave home when you weren't of legal age?" But I was emancipated at the age of fifteen so my parents could get me away from them. They did let me stick around for another year, as long as I paid rent. So I worked at fast-food places and dealt drugs till the day God spoke to me through that Ouija board.

It sounds totally crazy, I know, but it gets even better. Remember what God told me about bringing unity, healing marriages, and being a father to many?

For the next seventeen years, I would walk through everything that was opposite of what God called me. I watched my daughter die in my arms during a season in which I was praying for sick babies and all of them were being healed. Every relationship I had was destroyed. Marriage after marriage ended in divorce with the mother taking my children and disappearing.

In those days I was a deliverance minister and pastor—but I was the poster child for deliverance. I had come out of witchcraft and satanism, so once the deliverance ministers got ahold of me, I gave them a reason to do what they did. I was the experiment and they needed to deliver me of all those demons. Sounded good at the time, but unfortunately, it just twisted the image of God even more in my mind.

You see, when you are told you have a demon because you are a terrible sinner, it is only going to make you perform more to be right with God. Religion got ahold of me through the deliverance ministry, and I projected the same religiosity upon my family. If you didn't measure up, then God was angry with you. Every act of self-sabotage in my life was seen as the discipline of the Lord. I viewed the Father as an angry, wrathful God who only kept me around because Jesus was pleading with Him to give me another chance.

Relationships do not last long when you carry such self-hatred and self-rejection. If people tried to love me, I would find a way to get them to reject me. Of course I did not do this consciously; I just could not live up to all the false expectations I put upon myself. I was ousted from my biological family, the families I tried to build, and the church family. I was officially an outcast of society.

After seventeen years of rebuilding my life just to lose it all again, something happened: inner healing ministry came into my life.

I was now being told that not everything was a demon and that rejection was a lie I had believed.

I went through several inner-healing sessions and received a tremendous breakthrough. I began to see that the Father actually loved me.

This began the second phase of my journey, which would eventually lead me to pastor a revival in San Jose, California, in 2007. The Everlasting Gospel I had previously seen and all the inner healing I had received led me to that moment.

Everything seemed to be going well. I had influence and was seen as a father in the faith. I had a successful ministry with signs following. Our church was experiencing revival, so I began to seek out spiritual authority. I really wanted a father in my life, since all that I had walked through took place without discipleship; the Holy Spirit had taught me through the school of hard knocks.

The Lord brought me a spiritual father that year from a well-known ministry. We were sitting at a coffee shop chatting one day when he asked me, "Who are you? Who are you in God?"

I talked for the next twenty minutes about being a forerunner, an apostle, a revivalist. He patiently waited for me to finish and then said, "Well, that is nice to know what you are called to do—but who are you?"

I had no answer.

He comforted me and told me to go home and just pray about it. I headed home, feeling completely unworthy of being a pastor who was overseeing a move of God.

"I am not qualified!" I yelled. "I do not even know who I am!"

I wanted to quit the ministry that day. As I sat sobbing, totally discouraged, I had a vision:

I saw all of my faults, failures, and sins pass before me. I said, "Lord, I thought You forgave me of these things! You're not supposed to remember my sins anymore!"

I heard the Lord laugh and say, "Look again."

I looked and I saw the Father's affirmation through all the seasons where I believed I had failed Him.

He was smiling, with a look that said, *this is My son, in whom I am well pleased.*

He said, "Son, I called you as a grace bearer. All that you walked through was the infirmities of the people. Now you understand why you walked through these contradictions."

He then said, "No matter how much I tell My children that I love them, they really do not understand this until I have proven it to them. This requires failure to know My faithfulness."

I was stunned! Another veil was torn that day and another revelation of identity began to emerge for me. But the journey had just begun.

A year later in 2008, our church split and everything was destroyed. Another marriage had failed, and I was seen as an impostor. Before long, I found myself in yet another relationship.

My reputation is already destroyed, so why not just do it again? I thought. So I married the woman I was seeing and we moved out of state to start fresh.

The first year of marriage was difficult. I was again subconsciously trying to get her to leave me. In my mind I was not worthy of love. But my wife wouldn't leave; she refused to agree with the lies I had believed.

Nine months into my new marriage and still feeling the regret and loss of the church I previously pastored, I received a phone call from a dear friend in Washington state. I had been ministering to her for years and we were talking about prophetic ministry. She had never prophesied before, so I told her to practice on me.

As she stepped out in faith, asking the Lord for a word of prophecy for me, there was silence for a moment. Then she said, "God doesn't regret your past. Why do you?"

The encounter I'd had two years earlier, when God spoke to me about being a grace bearer, was being spoken afresh.

A few months later, a move of God broke out in Amarillo, Texas. I had stepped through the pain and the lies and was exploding with new vision. My marriage began to soar, and my wife and I began to see eye-to-eye like never before.

Little did I know, I would be walking through many more losses and betrayal before it was over.

A few years later, I was falsely accused of a crime, thrown into jail, and beaten half to death. But that led to a revival in two jails and a prison.

Seventeen months later I was vindicated and released, I saw another truth of sonship that would rip away another layer of self-protection.

What had once traumatized me was now destroying trauma itself. The pieces of the puzzle had come together, and what I had been forerunning would now bear fruit—not just for myself, but for many.

I no longer have regrets! I have now been happily married to my wife, Shauna, for twelve years; our marriage is beautiful and our family is stable. We have two handsome boys who are smart, compassionate, and full of love. We travel full-time in a motorhome covered in solar panels, ministering all over America in homes, churches, and anyplace else the Lord leads us. I no longer try to practice what I preach; I preach what I have practiced.

Everywhere we have gone, families and marriages have been impacted. Unity and love have been the fruits, with grace and sonship as the revelation.

This book is not a teaching I heard about or a doctrine I have studied. This is my life and testimony. But I did not receive it alone; the few who believed in me drew it out of me. We walked it out together and proved the fruit of the Everlasting Gospel of Jesus Christ.

As you gaze into the mysteries of Christ in this book, realize you are hidden within its pages. Some chapters will feel like a struggle, hard to grasp with the natural mind. But it is important to deal a mortal blow to opinion in order to manifest dominion. As Paul said, the natural man cannot understand the things of God, because they are spiritually discerned. Discernment is only as clear as how you see the Father's expression in the midst of your failures.

We tend to cling to what we have known, to what is familiar. But if you will allow your mind to simply drink and not think, then what does not make sense will be sensed experientially in who you were before you were formed in the womb. What I have walked out through the valley of the shadow of death has brought life that is now written down for you.

This is a love story about the Father and us as sons. We came from the bosom of the Father and were manifested as the Son. It is a game changer when you know that the Father did not just roll the dice hoping we would figure it all out, hoping we would make it back to heaven. We were foreordained for love! A love unfolding within His body that would expand everything we knew as spirit before time began. The Gospel is a revelation, a mystery—and this mystery is us hidden in Him.

I have found a heartbeat to the way revelation knowledge flows. It comes first to break our conclusions off of us by blowing our minds into another realm where we can't understand, but we must stand *under* the place where reason is treason in the law of the Spirit of Life. Once the mind has submitted to the unknown, then you will realize you were always known in Him. Practical application will then sweep through you, and all the pieces of the puzzle will make sense.

The chapters of this book will stretch you beyond thinking and then will swoop back down to reveal understanding. As my chaos became clarity, so will yours. And clarity is realized from eternity and the purpose for which you were sent.

I will use terminology you might not be familiar with, so let me explain a few phrases you will hear often through this book. The term "human experience" is used to describe the reality that you are not a human having a spiritual experience but a spirit having a human experience. The "timeline version of you" is another example of how you did not originate here on Planet Earth but came from God as spirit.

Mysteries from God's point of view are limited by human language and better experienced then explained, yet there is a place for explanation to be the diving board into realization. There are appointed times in which Christ is revealed in us, so be patient with how this mystery unveils and re-read this book a few times over to see it fully.

I have traveled to many states and cities ministering the Everlasting Gospel, and everywhere I go I hear the same responses. People will tell me they did not understand a thing I was saying, but they witnessed to it in their spirits. I usually will hear back from these same people a few months later and they will tell me that they *encountered* the truth of what I was saying. It will cause your mind to tilt when you first hear it and will break the boxes where your mind has been confined to reason.

I am an uneducated man and do not claim any scholarly abilities in the way in which I see God. I can only share how this revelation came from my devastation and that it has brought reconciliation and restoration to many. I had one man tell me it went over his head and then returned to hover and activate his identity!

So strap in and get ready to go where the human mind cannot go—a place outside of time and space, where the Blood speaks your history in the testimony of God.

Chapter Two

Origin into a Beginning

"Now, Father, glorify Me together with Yourself, with the glory which I had with You before the world was."— John 17:5

As we venture into the unknown of this glory Jesus had with the Father before the world was, we must first define what "origin" is compared to a beginning, and why this is important to our spiritual journey and progress.

Jesus had already been ministering for three and a half years when he made the statement above. He had healed the sick, preached the Kingdom, and raised the dead. He had unlimited power at His fingertips, and yet He stilled needed another kind of glory in order to fulfill redemption. This glory He asked the Father for was a glory they shared before the world began. Jesus then begins to pray for unity after He encounters this "before-the-beginning glory."

I believe this glory is connected to our origin—the unity that humanity carried before we were human. This glory would be the intentions the Father had for us coming into a human experience. God so loved the world that He gave His only begotten Son. The Father's loving intentions for us are what motivated Him to send His Son. Did the Father foreknow all that would happen on Planet Earth before the beginning? Of course He did. And when the Father sent the Son, it happened in the Lamb slain from the foundation of the world (Revelation 13:8). That event, which was seen two thousand years ago, came from the unseen. The unity we had as the Body of Christ is what brought us into a beginning known as "God so loving the world." It was love that sent us as the many to manifest the one, Christ. This is our origin: pure love.

"The beginning" is known as the seventh day. This seventh day is where all the generations have been sealed together in the intentions of love. When we draw from the Kingdom of God within us, we are remembering the seventh day. Everything you will ever need for the human experience was built in this day, which is known as the day of redemption. When Jesus was sent in human form, He came fully equipped to overcome. Because the seventh-day carried the testimony of those who overcame as a multi-membered body, Jesus could pull this into remembrance through the Father's affirmation.

Knowing that we were sent in the same way Jesus was sent means that just like Him, we were willing to come here, all in agreement together because of love. Why is this so important? Because this means that all we walk through on Planet Earth is being worked for good because we agreed with love. That means no more regret, no more self-pity, and no more confusion. We can rest and only do what we see the Father doing from a work that was us in the Father, known as "the beginning." We are not victims of circumstance; we are indestructible.

The game-changer here is that we are not waiting for God to *do* something before we can *be* something. We were always a family, and we came as a family. We have always been the household of faith, and Jesus came in the unity of our faith. This is how we can be vulnerable with one another. We are not strangers to one another because we made a covenant together and had a book written.

We built a house together in the beginning that would hold the book of our memories for us to find our lives again, after they'd been hidden in one another. As we continue to unfold this chapter, I will give many illustrations and scriptures that will help you grasp this glorious mystery that I call The Everlasting Gospel of Christ.

Jesus had the keys that enabled Him, as a man, to overcome every area in which mankind had fallen short. He knew who He was, and He knew where He came from. Modern-day Christianity has only seen the earthly view of redemption—from the outside in—when it comes to the purpose of the Father sending His Son.

Generations of believers have strived to attain victory in walking as Christ walked, but no one has yet put on what Jesus promised we would. His prayer for unity has not manifested in the church because we have been limited to a time-and-space perspective. Seeing Jesus only as an individual man is just one side of the Gospel. The fruit of unconditional love in a multi-membered body is the heart of the matter. This is the love that helps us to remember unity in the body of Christ.

We are told in Colossians 3 to set our minds on things above. Paul also tells us that we are to have the mind of Christ. What does this heavenly perception look like? Since God commanded the end from the beginning (Isaiah 46:10), we must see our lives from that perspective. Is it possible to only do what we see the Father doing? Definitely! We just need to learn to see things from God's point of view.

This fellowship with the mystery of Christ is an other-worldly journey into the very purpose of Him being sent and from whence He came. We know He came from Heaven, right? But it is deeper than the *place* He came from; it is a *state of being*. This chapter will focus on our invitation into thinking on heavenly things and the intentions of the Father in the life of Jesus, as well as our lives in Him as the multi-membered body of Christ. So let's begin!

Remembrance

In John 17, Jesus prays a prayer of remembrance. He asks for the glory He had with the Father before the beginning of the world. Jesus needed this reality to be realized in His human experience. Why did He need this remembrance of who He was before the beginning? The same reason we need it: to discern identity in the midst of resistance. He was about to go to the cross and would need the Father's understanding in order to endure all he was about to go through without offense or resistance. The carnal mind projects the illusion of death, but the spiritual mind realizes the reality of life as spirit.

He would also need all of His body, known as the household of faith or the many as One New Man, with Him in this transaction. Reconciliation is about awakening the reality of being in Him—not being reconnected, as though we were separated. Since God is outside of time and space, our faith was authored and finished before we even began this journey into a timeline human experience. Ephesians 1:4 tells us that we were chosen in Him before the foundation of the world.

This glory Jesus was reaching for in His prayer to the Father was us already in Him before the world was. His prayer for unity was not a hope for the future, but a declaration of our origin and the intention on which we agreed before the world was. Jesus came to Earth, not to send us after He died and rose again, but to remind us that we were sent as He is.

There are many scriptures that point to our pre-existence with God. Many through the ages have attempted to present this revelation only to end up indoctrinating it. This has caused much debate and division within the Body of Christ when the purpose of pre-existence is really about love and unity.

Genesis 1 gives us a glimpse into the beginning of the heavens and the earth. Not much is known today of God's intentions before the beginning—and this is what the unity of the faith is all about. To know the "why" behind the "what" is the posture of knowing the mind of Christ or the intentions of the Father.

Knowing intentions frees us from performance and self-effort, enabling grace to abound. The love and compassion that Jesus walked in could not be offended, no matter who was coming against Him. Can you imagine what it would be like to be unoffendable, no matter what is happening around you? To be asleep in a boat during a storm and not be moved because you understand the purposes of the Father in the midst of resistance? Everything God made or manifested in the beginning came from an intention *before* the beginning. In order for us to understand intentions in the glory we had before the world was, let us reflect on its explanation in the beginning.

It is not "the beginning of time," as we have been taught. It is the beginning of a three-dimensional realm of natural and spiritual. As we were chosen in Him before the beginning, what we were doing together was a glory that bore *the fruit of* a beginning. Paul tells us that we go from glory to glory; this did not begin in your human life. Humanity is but one kind of glory in an infinite journey we have had together before the beginning. The heavens and the earth are spirit manifested in visible form. We as spirits are not reduced to a third dimension, but what we built as a beginning is one of many dimensions in which we have journeyed.

While Genesis lays out six days during which God worked before He rested, scripture also tells us God also commanded the end from the beginning. So was God working during those six days—or was He unveiling what He had already done? Could it be that the Father was making visible what was already complete in an invisible form from a place of rest? Is the seventh day really when God rested from His works, or could the seventh day be a completed work on which all creation manifested?

Thus, the heavens and the earth were finished, and all the host of them. And on the seventh day God ended his work which he had made; and he rested on the seventh day from all his work which he had made. And God blessed the seventh day and sanctified it: because that in it he had rested from all his work which God created and made. These are the generations of the heavens and of the earth when they were created, in the day that the LORD God made the earth and the heavens (Genesis 2:1-4).

Hidden within the seventh day is every generation of Heaven and Earth. This is not linear time that we are dealing with; it is an all-knowing and all-powerful God unveiling what has always been known. Let us break this down a little more by defining the words "created" or "made" in the above scripture. We must be careful not to reduce the image of what God did to creating something from nothing. While we as humans might create something from nothing, divinity cannot follow the same rule: *So God created (bara) man in*

*his own image, in the image of God created
(bara) he him; male and female created (bara)
he them (Genesis1:27).*

Bara is a verb and is usually translated as
"create." To really understand what this word
means let us look at another passage where it
is used.

*Why do you scorn my sacrifice and offering
that I prescribed for my dwelling? Why do you
honor your sons more than me by fattening
(bara) yourselves on the choice parts of every
offering made by my people Israel?* (1 Samuel
2:29).

The word "fattening" in the passage above is
the Hebrew word *bara*. The noun form of this
verb is *beriya* and can be found in Genesis
41:4: "And the cows that were ugly and gaunt
ate up the seven sleek, fat cows." The word
"fat" is the Hebrew word *beriya*. Therefore, the
word *bara* does not mean "to create," but "to
fatten." The Hebrew language actually has no

word that means "to create" in the sense of making something out of nothing. There are also other meanings of this word *bara*, such as "to squeeze out," "to ordain," "to beget," or "to manifest." Now these are the unused roots, but they are attached to this word in the Hebrew. "So God (fattened, manifested, ordained) man in his own image, in the image of God fattened he him; male and female fattened he them."

Since God is omniscient, knowing all things, how can He come up with something not previously known? To have a pre-thought would make Him less than God, and to create something out of nothing would negate His divinity. This raises another question: How does an all-knowing God know all things, yet never come to the end of Himself? Think about it. There is no end or beginning to the infinite nature of God, yet He knows all things. Personally, I believe God hides things from Himself and within Himself that are unveiled in us.

Matthew 24:36 tells us that no one knows the day nor the hour of Christ's return, not even the Son—only the Father. 1 Corinthians 2:10 tells us that the Spirit searches the deep things of God. Now we know God is One and He manifests as Father, Son, and Holy Spirit. Yet we can see the relationship in which the Godhead fellowships within His own mystery of searching Himself out, and yet knowing all things. We read in Colossians 3:4 that Christ, who is our life, will be revealed and we will be seen with Him. *We* are the mystery hidden within the Godhead. Our personalities are a part of God's own diversity that He hid within Himself. In order for us to honor one another as Christ has honored us, we must see ourselves as one with the Father as Christ did.

Let this mind be in you which was also in Christ Jesus, who, being in the form of God, did not consider it robbery to be equal with God, but made Himself of no reputation, taking the form of a bondservant, *and* coming in the likeness of men (Philippians 2:5-7).

We have the same mind as Jesus. Not only in our Christian walk, but also in our heavenly origin. When God was making Himself of no reputation, He became a man. Allowing this mind to be in us is confirming equality with God.

Some might be thinking it is heresy to claim equality with God, but we must understand the parallel between spirit and the finite human experience. Jesus said, "My Father is greater than I." This was as a man; the Father was greater than the Son. Yet Jesus also said, "My Father and I are one and the same." This was from the place of origin and spirit.

What does equality with God look like? The absence of insecurity, competition, and jealousy. To be godly in the very image of God as spirit has nothing to do with self-exaltation as a man; it simply means to look like Jesus.

Have you ever met a married couple in which the man made himself out to be superior to his wife? We would say this is a dysfunctional relationship and is doomed to fail. Realize that equality is the foundation of healthy relationships, and our equality with God is the foundation of our identity in Christ as sons and daughters.

We were chosen in Him before the beginning, and in the beginning, spirit morphed into a three-dimensional form. We have always been in the multi-membered Body of Christ. Jesus as our example put on spiritual amnesia and came to Earth. As He viewed life through the mindset of humanity, He reached for equality with the Father as the Son. He grew in wisdom, favor, and stature with God and with man. He came into remembrance by revelation of who He was before He was formed in the womb (Jeremiah 1:5). He siphoned His Identity from eternity into His human consciousness by only receiving how the Father saw Him as the Son.

He demonstrated all of this so we could remember!

"Truly, truly, I say to you, the Son can do nothing of Himself, unless it is something He sees the Father doing; for whatever the Father does, these things the Son also does in like manner. For the Father loves the Son and shows Him all things that He Himself is doing" (John 5:19-20).

It was the Father doing the works through Jesus. And these works were finished from the foundation of the world (Hebrews 4:3). The posture for this echo of a finished work to flow into time to redeem the time came from the realization of being fully loved by the Father. When you know origin, you realize unconditional love. When we believe we came from Earth, we will promote the need to measure up in being spiritual. We as believers try to obey to be approved, yet Jesus modeled obedience *because* He was approved. His approval was not based on performance, but on the nature of the Father and a completed work. Did Jesus come to redeem victims of circumstance, or did He come to awaken sons and daughters?

Awake O sleeper and Christ will give you light! (Ephesians 5:14).

What light will Christ give us when we awake? John 1:4 says, "In Him was life and the life was the light of men." He came to wake us up and reconcile who we were in Him into our human experience. The life is in the blood, and this life is you who were in Him as a multi-membered body.

But what about accepting Christ in your hearts to be saved? While we look at the outward manifestation or human response to being saved, we judge that "Christ just came into my heart." Is God doing a new thing or is there nothing new under the sun? It is new to us *in our human experience*. As 2 Corinthians 5:17 tells us, all things are new and all things are of

God. "Being saved" is new to our human consciousness because we are now awakened to the truth. Paul spoke of an appointed time in which "Christ would be revealed in me." The next time you read the scripture that says Jesus stands at the door and knocks, realize He is knocking from the inside—for the Kingdom is within you.

Here is the mind of Christ that is our reality as spirit but which must be remembered in our minds: God had a human experience as Christ. He came from a seventh-day reality in which all the generations of His body were sanctified. He put on the blindfold of man's thinking and joined it to how the Father saw Him from the beginning. With every temptation, He took our perceptions and conclusions and shifted them into how the Father sees us. He came to awaken us to who we have always been in Him.

His death on the cross would be the greatest example of love, proving that God was not wrath but love. Golgotha, the place of a skull, would be the undoing of a twisted imagery of our identity from the tree of knowledge of good and evil. Now that we see Christ in a new light and our participation with Him from a seventh-day finished work, let us now dig into Genesis in which we as spirit are hidden.

In the beginning God created the heaven and the earth. And the earth was without form, and void; and darkness was upon the face of the deep. And the Spirit of God moved upon the face of the waters. And God said, let there be light: and there was light. And God saw the light, that it was good: and God divided the light from the darkness. And God called the light Day, and the darkness he called Night. And the evening and the morning were the first day (Genesis 1:1-5).

While there are layers of interpretation to the scriptures, I will choose the approach that will best benefit identity in Christ. In 2 Corinthians 4:18, Paul tells us that what is seen originates with what is unseen. Just as faith is the substance of things hoped for and the evidence of things not seen, so the ways of God are in the unseen and the acts of God become visible. Jesus told the religious leaders of His day that the scriptures testify of Him. To get to the heart of the matter, we must look beyond the surface of natural creation and listen to the groaning within creation for the manifest sons of God.

In Genesis 1, we can see us in Him within the heavens and the earth. We hear the saying, "When you die, you will go to Heaven," and we just agree to this. Yet Heaven is not really a place you go; it is the spiritual state you are in. It is not good news that declares we must die in order to enter in, for the Kingdom is within you.

The "beginning" is not only a three-dimensional realm as we see it; it also means "first fruits." Dig a little deeper and you will find that the masculinity of God is emphasized here. We can connect this with terms like "the seed of Christ," or "incorruptible seed" (see 1 Peter 1:23). Go a little further in Genesis 1 and you will see the earth was without form, which is better translated as "hidden."

Remember, the Word was made flesh, yet Christ was always here. We also see that the Spirit was hovering over the face of the deep and there was darkness. Since darkness and light are the same to God, darkness does not necessarily mean it is evil. God is surrounded with dark clouds; this points to the deep things or mysteries of God not yet revealed.

Day One of creation is known as what is going on in the heavens or spirit realm. We see God separating light from darkness and calling it "the first day." But this was not a day of the week, from which we view life from linear time. In fact, it wasn't till the fourth day that the sun, moon, stars, seasons, and times began to manifest. So how can a day have light and darkness without a sun or a moon? When we cross-reference the dividing of light and darkness with Ephesians 1:10, we find a glorious truth.

... that in the dispensation of the fullness of the times He might gather together in one all things in Christ, both which are in heaven and which are on earth—in Him (Ephesians 1:10).

While Heaven and Earth can mean either us as spirit or us in visible human form, so light and darkness on the first day of creation reveals the same. Who we are as spirit, sealed until the day of redemption in these vessels of clay, is also seen as darkness. Paul said it this way in 2 Corinthians 4:7: "We have this treasure in earthen vessels." Isaiah calls it "treasures in darkness" (Isaiah 45:3).

So we have a dispensation of the fullness of time in which we are awakened to the reality of what we are as spirit. We were divided in the beginning by the tree of knowledge, preventing true identity from being touched after the twisted mind fell asleep. The emphasis in Ephesians 1:10 is that everything now being reconciled was always within Christ—never outside of Him.

This is liberating! This is where we begin to get a glimpse of hope! The true image of the Father begins to take shape in our human consciousness, and we realize how Jesus stood complete in the Father.

Let there be light! The actual passage reads, "Be light!" And now comes the proclamation into all creation of the manifest sons of God known as the spiritual Christ in Ephesians 1:4. Can you see the Father's intentions becoming clearer? Day One of creation is about us being sealed till the day of redemption by the Holy Spirit. We see the Spirit hovering over this darkness or mystery of Christ in us hidden until the day of redemption. The face coming up from the deep is also us as the spiritual Christ bringing forth expression through the Spirit hovering.

Spirit is also known as light. Light can be related to atoms and subatomic particles that are made of light and move at the speed of light. Imagine Spirit moving so fast it cannot be seen till it slows down to a visible state. This is the face of future humanity gazing into a human experience from the other side. Let's see our face in scripture.

When He prepared the heavens, I was there,

When He drew a circle on the face of the deep (Proverbs 8:27).

And God said, let there be a firmament in the midst of the waters, and let it divide the waters from the waters (Genesis 1:6).

Again, the second day is still dealing with the intentions and movement of Spirit. The word *firmament* means "arch." It also means "heavenly bodies." And since out of our bellies flow rivers of living water, we can see again the dividing of who we are in Christ from the blindfolded human experience. In Hebrews

4:12 we are told that the Word of God is sharper than any two-edged sword. It divides between soul and spirit. Is God dividing, or has He broken down the middle wall that has prevented the peace of God from surpassing our own understanding? The Word is a two-edged sword—two voices becoming one. It is God's voice and our voice as one voice, known as the sound of many waters.

His Word, which was also in the beginning (as John 1 tells us), is removing what has divided our perception. While the two trees in the garden parallel the two sides of the brain, the revelation of reconciliation enables us to live from the experiential knowledge of God known as the memory of who we were. We have always been the many as the one new man! To see more sides to this revelation of our origin, we will look at two scriptures that take us back to the beginning.

In the beginning was the Word, and the Word was with God, and the Word was God. The same was in the beginning with God. All things were made by him; and without him was not anything made that was made. In him was life; and the life was the light of men. And the light shineth in darkness; and the darkness comprehended it not (John 1:1-5).

In the beginning, we were living epistles of Christ (2 Cor.3:3). This light of men was the many as one new man, which declares, "BE LIGHT!" This is not a light that requires *doing* something to *be* something; your light is veiled by reducing yourself to human history. Jesus said, "Be perfect, even as your Father in Heaven is perfect" (Matt.5:48). As we transition from trying to attain into realizing who we are in our origin, we will experience the reality of what it means to just *be*. Jesus modeled this by only doing what He saw the Father doing. He was wrapped up in the reality of just being, and the Father echoed that finished work right through Him.

To the crowds of people, it seemed God was doing a new thing! Yet the new thing is only our human awareness of what was always there— just hidden. "All my days were written in the book" (Psalm 139:16). It is mistaken identity through the ego of the Tree of Knowledge that presents the illusion of separation and lack. Unfortunately, the twenty-first-century church has been presenting redemption from Adam and Eve's perspective rather than the Father's through the eternal Christ.

The third scripture we need to look at is 1 John 1:1.

That which was from the beginning, which we have heard, which we have seen with our eyes, which we have looked upon, and our hands have handled, of the Word of life.

Not only were we in the book and in the Word from the beginning, but we handled eternal life. John gives us a picture here of how unity is realized. We have been on a long journey together. We made a covenant together, and we have given of ourselves to one another before time began. This is what it means to know no one after the flesh, but only by the Spirit. For our joy to be complete, we must realize we came from another realm, another state of being, and agreed to reunite here. Our fellowship is the communion of the Father and the Son—no separation! God is light and in Him is no darkness! Where are you? In Him before the foundation of the world.

If we say that we have fellowship with him, and walk in darkness, we lie, and do not have the truth (1 John1:6).

What does it mean to say we fellowship with Him and walk in darkness? It relates to believing lies and not seeing truth. This is the lie of separation, the slumber in which our eyes no longer see origin. We have reduced ourselves to a natural realm and have become entangled with the cares of this life. Living in the illusion of being mere humans has kept us in the lie that we are not in Him.

The blood of Jesus carries your life in the DNA of the Father. The very memories of God are our journey together into a visible state.

Without seeing the beginning, handling the word of life, and experiencing the Father and the Son, there can be no fellowship with one another. Unity is the fruit of identity, and identity is the fruit of communion with the Father and the Son. Communion is the fruit of revelation, and revelation lives outside of time in the eternity of God. That's why the scripture declares, "NOW faith is!"

When we experience a suddenly of God in our lives, these are memories inviting us into a greater place of unveiling the mysteries of heavenly ordination. "Before I formed you in the womb, you were ordained!" (Jeremiah 1:5). We came to Earth as Jesus did—from Heaven. When Jesus said, "As the Father has sent me,

I now send you," He was speaking from eternity into time, from spirit into humanity.

The Word of God is an encounter that reveals God in you and you in God. The Gospel of salvation is more than a general message of what He came to do for you.

... in whom ye also trusted, after that ye heard the word of truth, the gospel of your salvation: in whom also after that ye believed, ye were sealed with that Holy Spirit of promise (Ephesians 1:13).

Look at the progression of this verse. You trusted because you heard the truth, and that truth carried a testimony or testament. This testament is also known as the Gospel. The four gospels focus on the life, death, and resurrection of Christ. scripture also declares that the testimony of Jesus is the spirit of prophecy. We are called as living epistles that are read by others around us. When we add this up, we get a personalized revelation of our involvement of the purpose of God in our generation—in effect, the Gospel of salvation.

The above verse confirms that after all this, we believe and are sealed with the Holy Spirit of promise. We didn't *believe* first; we *trusted* first. We trusted Him in eternity, in our true identity. We believed as faith that framed the future human experience with our identity in the Word of God. We walked through time and heard our faith as spirit preaching the Gospel.

Yet when we were saved or awakened, we didn't necessarily understand this right away—probably not for years. But as we journey through this human experience with God, the facades begin to fall off. It is at this place that we begin to see our identity beyond the timeline. We see face-to-face and identify with the life of Jesus in the Father.

We are sealed till the day of redemption, which is the same day on which God rested from all His works. It is a day outside of time, which carries the complete works of God for our human experience. When our minds become renewed by revelation, we embrace our identity. It is here that true, living faith is expressed. This is where the promises of God become tangible reality.

And the scripture, foreseeing that God would justify the heathen through faith, preached before the gospel unto Abraham, saying, in thee shall all nations be blessed (Galatians 3:8).

The Gospel was first preached to Abraham. "Look at the stars Abraham; so shall your descendant be" (Genesis 15:5). This was the Gospel! Abraham was given the revelation of Christ, the genealogy, and his part to play in it. Abraham partnered with God to become the father of faith. Until we know who we are in Him from the foundation of the world, we will not be able to fully partner with Him in this parable version of ourselves.

Abraham did prophetic acts by offering Isaac as a sacrifice. He was embodying the Gospel, and because it involved Abraham, it was the gospel of his salvation as well as ours. We must go beyond the impersonal Gospel message into the eternal purpose of God in which we see and understand—I in Him and Him in me. There are natural life situations in which God has placed you that carry revelations of who you were before you were formed in the womb. As you gaze into the mysteries of heavenly perception, you will find God's design, His blueprint of your purpose and destiny. Every time you encounter God, you are remembering eternity.

To sum this up, I will speak plainly. In the first fruits of the masculinity of divinity, in the incorruptible seed of the Spiritual Christ, a house was built, eternal in the heavens and built from layers of spirit memories. This manifested as Heaven and Earth. The visible human experience appeared without form yet was hidden in dark mysteries until Spirit slowed down and hovered. Our expression began to manifest as a face coming out of the depths of origin—humanity in a glorified state being proclaimed, "Be light!"

We agreed that who we are as light would walk through the lie of separation in our human counterpart, which would live in the illusion of darkness until the appointed time of awakening. This would prove pure love from eternity to unlock unconditional love in the timeline.

So, who were we before the beginning? Or as Daniel would say, before thrones were set up (Daniel 7:9)? While there is no language that can express what was before the beginning, I will do my best to bring the heart of the matter. Jesus said, "I tell you earthly things and you don't believe; how shall I tell you heavenly things?" (John 3:12). Since the Heaven of heavens cannot contain Him, I will use parables to bridge eternity with the beginning.

Paul called it "comparing spiritual things with spiritual"; there is no earthly comparison to the plain speech of God.

We are told to pray for life to be "on Earth as it is in Heaven." We must realize that the seen reflects the unseen. This means that Heaven is what earth looks like through spiritual eyes. What can be compared are earthly things because we can compare what is on earth to what is in heaven. But where there is no earthly grid, eternity comes in. On Earth we have an external view, and in Heaven there is an internal view.

Heaven and Earth have a beginning, known as the first fruits of all humanity hidden in Spirit, which then emerges through the human journey.

Eternity or origin is before all of this, and yet it exists simultaneously because there is no time. So who you were *before* time and who you are *in* time coexist. But for the sake of our finite minds, we will use bridges of earthly things to attempt to look into the face-to-face reality that has no face in true form. God in His true form has no form and looks like nothing. Why? Because no-thing can be compared to Him. You are not going to a place called eternity; you are made of eternity as spirit.

Spirit is singular in eternity, while the visible human experience is lived through a cracked mirror of duality. Therefore, we struggle with light and darkness, good and evil. Yet from the Father's perspective, everything He made was good. And He will work all things together for good!

Everything Jesus did in His ministry on Earth, He pulled from the seventh-day finished work. This is all the generations from a glorified state before the human echo, if I can say it that way. This is what differentiates how Jesus only did what the Father was doing from a finished work. He needed another glory from before the world was made. This glory would unlock intentions that would enable Jesus to enter the rest of the seventh day.

His sonship in the seventh day was remembered as He grew in wisdom, favor, and stature. He remembered what it meant to be light in Genesis 1 when He was on the Mount of Transfiguration. It was a remembrance that would posture Him in order to shift His human mind into the Father's perspective. He had to see the glory that would be revealed in order to endure the present suffering (Romans 8:18). But though He saw the outcome that was already foreordained in the seventh day, He still needed to know the intentions that only come from origin.

This is the "why" behind the "what"! It is one thing to know you are sitting in a house that has been built, and quite another thing to know why it was built. It is not enough to know what you are called to do; you must know who you are in the purposes of the Father. This glory before the world began was and is our unity. It was our holy conversation (Philippians 3:20). It was the book of remembrance (Malachi3:16)—the very blueprint of pure love in the multi-membered body that would build a house known as the future human experience.

No matter how much we know and believe in the finished works of God, without knowing intention we will still strive religiously to put it on from a place of lack. We will attempt to attain it rather than unveil it. To remove the veil is to realize our origin in the communion we had in the Father before the beginning—the glory we had before the world was. Knowing intentions is everything! When we do not know someone's intentions, we are suspicious and self-protective. We fear loss in this place because we have not been made perfect in love. Most of our fears in life did not originate with traumatic events, as we suppose. It is the lack of understanding the purpose of the event that keeps us in a tailspin of despair.

In the next chapter, we will continue this journey into origin by looking at different parables in scripture of who we were in former glories before the beginning. And don't worry: we will have a chapter that will tie together intentions during contradictions that will aid you in entering the rest of God in this life.

Many have not even considered seeing redemption from outside of time or being able to see themselves in the image of God outside their human experience. But this changes everything in the way we live and interact with God in prayer. The way we see each other allows us to enter a place where unconditional love is possible. While this chapter might seem mystical, our identity has been hidden in a God who lives outside of time and space. Getting His point of view is the game changer that allows grace to abound where believers everywhere have struggled for so long.

Chapter Three

Former Glories

And I saw another angel fly in the midst of heaven, having the everlasting gospel to preach unto them that dwell on the earth, and to every nation, and kindred, and tongue, and people (Revelation 14:6)

Before we venture down this rabbit hole of multiple versions or former glories, let us break out of the box concerning angels and who they are.

I was always told that angels were created to serve God, and we were created to love God. And yes, on one level of perception, angels are sent to help us and labor with us. But what does the word "angel" mean in Hebrew?

Psalm 8:5 tells us man was made or manifested as "a little lower than the angels." That word "angels" in Hebrew is *mê·'ĕ·lō·hîm,* meaning "God." While there are many different references to angels as messengers that show them as less than God, we must also consider how we entertain strangers as angels in human form. I do not want to build a box or conclusion here; I would rather break previous conclusions we have had when it comes to defining angels.

Many would say "the angel of the Lord" refers to Jesus in another form before the Word was made flesh. But since we were chosen in Him before humanity manifested, we also are part of this angelic expression. So if "angel" in the Hebrew can mean "God," and in the Greek can mean "messenger," then we can see that God was sent as a messenger. We also see Jesus equating humans as angels in Matthew 22:30:

For in the resurrection they neither marry, nor are given in marriage, but are as the angels of God in heaven.

Many of the illustrations in scripture concerning angels have hidden within them our interaction with the Father.

Are they not all ministering spirits, sent forth to minister for them who shall be heirs of salvation? (Hebrews 1:14).

Hebrews 1 can appear on the surface to make angels separate from the human race, yet when we look deeper, we can see God is continually exceeding Himself in the unveiling of manifold Wisdom. Since angels desire to gaze into salvation, could it be that we were gazing into another glory from one form into another? Could my baptism of the Holy Spirit and speaking in tongues here on Planet Earth simply be the foundation of "on Earth as it is in Heaven"?

If I speak with the tongue of men and of angels but have not love ... (1 Corinthians 13:1).

God's love here is in the absence of fear, known as perfect love. We do not love ignorantly, but from a place of purpose and intention. Knowing security in Christ requires us to discern our journey. It just so happens that our journey did not begin in human form, but long ago in eternity. I believe that these ministering spirits known as angels sent to awaken us is us. Our identity in Christ echoing into our human consciousness.

There are so many angels mentioned in the Book of Revelations. Over and over again, we hear the term, "another angel came." They are blowing trumpets and pouring out vials. Could it be *us in another form? Were we beside ourselves,* echoing into the spiritual Christ that would appear in human form? Could it be happening before time as well as in our human minds simultaneously? That who we were in one dimension is blowing the trumpet of victory into our human consciousness. Our human life feels like we just got the breakthrough—but who we *were* blew that trumpet eons ago, and we are now hearing it at the appointed time.

This human formation from an angelic race would be the invitation into sonship. Were we sons and daughters? I believe that though we were all things already in Him, mysteries did not begin with our human experience. While God in His divinity conceals a matter, we as kings search it out. Proverbs 25:2 declares:

It is the glory of God to conceal a thing: but the honor of kings *is* to search out a matter.

Since we are His glory concealed, and the word *honor* means "glory," could we be unveiling as a mystery what has been continually sought out? In Chapter Two I spoke of God hiding different dimensions of Himself from Himself within Himself so as never to come to the end of Himself. By doing this, He can know all things and yet never end. For everything He knows is in a present place outside of time and space.

Let me use an example of human relationship to paint a picture. Falling in love with another person and continuing that pursuit of love has two different facets—mystery and spontaneity. What stirs us to pursue is the mystery and the desire to unveil and get to know the person we are in love with. Imagine if the moment you met the person you would marry; you knew everything about them before walking it out together. You would see every weakness, argument, and doubt. You might not want to pursue if you already had a preconceived idea and conclusion about that person. In fact, our conclusion about one another is where relationship ends.

Have you ever been told a lie about someone you didn't know—and then when you met them, you had walls up to protect yourself? Mystery is vital for us to stay in a *now* embrace without judgment.

The other facet is spontaneity. Being spontaneous keeps things fresh and keeps us fascinated with the person we love. It creates an atmosphere that deepens bonds and prevents stagnation. Many of the boxes we have put God in have been conclusions that have appeared as places of arrival, in which the life-giving Spirit is no longer present in our experience. God in His divinity does not need a journey of relationship to know the end of the matter—yet the finite experience or veiled mystery allows covenant relationship with us to become the backbone or proof of unconditional love in action. Did God conceal Himself within us, that the Father might pull from His bosom the multi-membered body that would put on kingship from one glory just to gaze into sonship in another?

The angel in Revelation14 proclaiming the everlasting Gospel is us in angelic form. Colossians 1:23 says, "If ye continue in the faith grounded and settled and be not moved away from the hope of the gospel, which ye have heard, and which was preached to every creature which is under heaven...."

The Everlasting Gospel was already in us when we were born as humans. It is the house that Wisdom built and is known as the seventh day which is now being revealed from the foundation of the world. We will get into how we were the incarnation of Wisdom a little later, but for now, let us continue to look into the unveiling of manifold Wisdom.

This angel in Revelation 14 is an unveiling from two other parable forms in Revelation 10 and 12. So let's go back and see where we are hidden in the scriptures.

And I saw another mighty angel come down from heaven, clothed with a cloud: and a rainbow was upon his head, and his face was as it were the sun, and his feet as pillars of fire: And he had in his hand a little book open: and he set his right foot upon the sea, and his left foot on the earth, And cried with a loud voice, as when a lion roareth: and when he had cried, seven thunders uttered their voices. And when the seven thunders had uttered their voices, I was about to write: and I heard a voice from heaven saying unto me, seal up those things which the seven thunders uttered and write them not (Revelation 10:1-4).

For the sake of our finite understanding, I will introduce this angel as *us*, the many as one. Yet it is a generic version that has yet to unveil the expression of sonship in the human experience. This angel is clothing himself with a cloud. This cloud is seen in Hebrews 12:1 as the cloud of witnesses. We can see here the labor that is known as the works of God leading up to a seventh-day finished work. We, the many as the one in angelic form, were placing a future version of ourselves upon ourselves—the sound of a glorified humanity before man ever walked it out in the physical. The very memory of a future that guaranteed prophetic fulfillment before prophecy was ever spoken through the prophets.

The next thing we see is that the angel's face was as the sun and he had an open book in his hand. Now as we journey into Revelation 12, we will find a woman who is "clothed with the sun." So who we were as the angel with the face of the sun is about to unveil into a woman giving birth to the human experience. This angel holding the book is the masculinity of God, which will become intimate with the femininity of God, known as the woman with the twelve stars.

Prophecy is you kissing your identity in the future. Yet that future is really a memory of a dimension you built before time to guarantee the end result. The open book is the conversation we had together in the Ancient of Days before thrones were set up.

Then they that feared the LORD spake often one to another: and the LORD hearkened, and heard it, and a book of remembrance was written before him for them that feared the LORD, and that thought upon his name. And they shall be mine, saith the LORD of hosts, in that day when I make up my jewels; and I will spare them, as a man spareth his own son that serveth him. Then shall ye return, and discern between the righteous and the wicked, between him that serveth God and him that serveth him not (Malachi 3:16-18).

This book carries the intentions of God being conversed in the fear of the Lord. We must understand that the fear of the Lord has nothing to do with being afraid of God. Isaiah 11:3 tells us that the fear of the Lord does not judge by outward appearance but by righteousness within. Since we are the righteousness of God in Christ and we were chosen in Him before time began, we can then see how intention led to Wisdom building a house. In order to build a future human experience that carried the proclamation of being complete in Christ, it would have to be built without human hands. The book is a blueprint of the Father's intentions that was our conversation in covenant relationship.

Now, this angel holding an open book cries out as a lion roaring. In Revelation 5, we see Christ the Lion as a King holding a book or scroll that is sealed. The book is sonship being broken open through a kingship in a former glory. Remember, you are sealed until the day of redemption by the Holy Spirit (Ephesians 4:30). And in John 1:12-13, you stepped into sonship in the seventh day. Your decision to be sent as Jesus was sent was not based on flesh and blood, but the will of God. Our striving to attain begins to break off when we realize all our members were written in the book.

And no man in heaven, nor in earth, neither under the earth, was able to open the book, neither to look thereon. And I wept much, because no man was found worthy to open and to read the book, neither to look thereon (Revelation 5:3-4.

The book can only be opened by the same standard with which it was written. We spoke one to another, and a book of remembrance was written. It has always been *us* and *we!* Individualized Christianity has been divisive and has diluted identity in the multi-membered body. But we are accepted in the beloved! We are baptized into one body! Only the corporate body of Christ will know completeness and worthiness to break open the unity of the saints from before the beginning.

There are a few more pieces to the puzzle as we read on in Revelation 10:6-7:

And sware by him that liveth for ever and ever, who created heaven, and the things that therein are, and the earth, and the things that therein are, and the sea, and the things which are therein, that there should be time no longer: But in the days of the voice of the seventh angel, when he shall begin to sound, the mystery of God should be finished, as he hath declared to his servants the prophets.

The voice of the seventh angel is the proclamation of God sanctifying the seventh day and all the generations of the heavens and the earth. It is an outside-of-time, completed work. Our human experience is a slowed-down, instant replay of an "on Earth as it is in Heaven" reality. How do we live in a state in which there shall be time no longer? Only the present is the place without time. Now faith is!

The present embrace is where we access this completed grace that we co-labored with in Christ before time began. We took our plain speech before time and formed it into layers of parables or holograms in the generations to spark eternal triggers, that we might wake up in remembrance of the purpose for which we were sent.

We as kings, as the one new man in the King, gazed into sonship in a book of the holy intentions of God. Seeing that even before time began there would be an appointed time in which Christ would be revealed in me (Galatians 1:16). Paul the Apostle speaks of this unveiling as a mystery hidden since the foundation of the world.

Unto me, who am less than the least of all saints, is this grace given, that I should preach among the Gentiles the unsearchable riches of Christ; And to make all men see what is the fellowship of the mystery, which from the beginning of the world hath been hid in God, who created all things by Jesus Christ: To the intent that now unto the principalities and powers in heavenly places might be known by the church the manifold wisdom of God, According to the eternal purpose which he purposed in Christ Jesus our Lord: In whom we have boldness and access with confidence by the faith of him (Ephesians 3:8-12).

Our boldness and confidence come from former glories in which we walked in His faith as co-laborers to encode the natural physical world with clues in the form of signs, wonders, encounters, visions, and dreams. This grace Paul speaks of receiving as predestination in what was completed from the very thought of God. The mystery of our identity in Him in eternity enables us to walk in grace here, hidden since the foundation of the world as Christ in you. Not only was Jesus revealed in Paul, but he also says it again in regard to preaching among the Gentiles.

That word "among" actually means "from within." In other words, Paul is preaching that which is within the Gentiles of the unsearchable riches of Christ. They are unsearchable by the natural mind, yet fully disclosed by the mind of Christ.

This brings us to the reality that the Church can make the manifold wisdom of God known to principalities and powers within the human race..

We have been speaking a lot about intentions, so let us go deeper. In connection to intention in the above passage we see the word "principality." The root word here is "principle" or "principles." Where my mind still thinks on carnal things, I need to put my mind above (Colossians3:1-2). When I know my origin as spirit, I will be able to bring my thoughts captive to the obedience of Christ (2 Corinthians10:3-5). And what is the outcome of the mind of Christ manifested in His body? The Father's intentions that manifest the manifold (or "many-folded") wisdoms or glories of your identity. Jesus makes this clear in John 8:14:

Jesus answered and said unto them, Though I bear record of myself, yet my record is true: for I know whence I came, and whither I go.

I believe that when Jesus tells them in verse 32 that they shall know the truth and the truth will set them free, it is based on the revelation of origin. We will go into practical application later in this book, but for now let us move on to another parable of a former glory!

I had an encounter in the seventh day. I was standing in a heavenly territory dressed as a king. A man walked in who looked familiar to me, but I couldn't place his face. This man began to speak to me of the wonders of God that I could not even comprehend. I became aware that this encounter was a memory of who I was before I was formed in the womb. I was a king, and this man standing in front of me was preaching the Gospel to me, inviting me into sonship. I was being invited into another realm called "Earth." He told me that I was called to be a son and that the kingship I currently walked in was only part of my identity. As I looked closer into this man's eyes, I realized it was me in a future human experience. I was as an angel gazing into salvation, which I could not comprehend. As my spirit agreed with my future self, I was ushered before the Throne.

Jesus my King had a new expression and persona I had never seen before. It was as though a new dimension of God was inviting me on a new adventure. Jesus looked at me with eyes of love, and He poured oil over my head. He then told me I would not directly remember this place once I stepped into time but that signs, wonders, and miracles would begin to trigger these eternal memories of my identity. He then brought out a treasure chest that had no latch or lock upon the lid. It was like a wax seal keeping the top on. Jesus then said, "This is everything you need for the journey. You are already complete, nothing lacking."

I asked the Lord, "How do I open it?"

He said, "It only opens through pressure. This will guarantee that nothing could ever be lost." I bowed before Him as He laid His hands upon me to commission me.

He then said, "The time will come when you will fully remember your identity. I will add sonship to the kingship that you presently carry. In the fullness of time, remembrance will release your territory I have given you in Heaven upon the earth. This will be seen as your life message."

Jesus then looked out among the other kings and lords. He shouted, "And who will go with him to help him remember who he was?"

Then Jesus reached inside me, pulled out a full-length mirror, and broke it on the ground. Many came forward and took a sliver of my mirror and placed it inside their spirits. As they were doing this, I heard Ephesians 1:18 spoken from the slivers of my broken imagery.

"Riches, glory, Inheritance!" spoken over and over again. I realized then when I have a word for people, it is coming from what we exchanged before time that manifests as inheritance in our human journey.

The Lord then made another request of those standing by. "And who will go and resist him, that the treasure chest might open?" I was stunned as one particular person came forward with such love in his eyes. He said, "I have agreed to be your enemy because I love you enough to see you fulfill your destiny."

This now made sense: when Jesus said to love your enemies, it's because they really are not enemies—they are there to confront the enemy in our own minds, which is the ego of man.

Jesus continued, "When others leave you and speak evil of you, realize I have called you to reconcile My body together. When they reject you, realize I have called you to affirm others. When division arises, remember I have called you to Planet Earth for the purpose of unity. All the opposites will present themselves to resist you, but I have set up your journey so you cannot fail. I have hidden My revelation within you and have tuned your spirit to respond to the truth every time a lie is presented." Jesus smiled and then kissed me on the forehead.

He spoke once more and said, "You have overcome because I have overcome. Every contradiction will be a steppingstone to unlock what I have placed within you." He then placed a garment upon me, and I was ushered through a portal into the timeline.

We must never despise the tough times we go through in our human experience. To count it all joy stems from knowing the intentions for which we were sent. As we journey together through the pages of this book, we will find divine remembrance that will lift the burdens of self-evaluation and self-condemnation. Our identity from eternity was sent into a timeline version of ourselves to unlock and prove eternal mysteries that could not be proven in a dimension of bliss. The truth of Godliness in the Godhead is proven in bodily form through contradictions.

Later on in the book we will focus upon the reality of sovereignty and divine contradictions needed to unlock the truth of who you have always been in Him. But before we can unpack this, we need some more parables of former glories.

Our Heavenly Father sees us as perfect and complete from a place of spirit. When the Father spoke at the baptism of Jesus, He said, "This is My Son in whom I am well pleased" (Matthew 3:17). Jesus had not yet been tested nor had He proven Himself, and yet, the Father saw Him as perfect. Isaiah 6 gives us a beautiful picture of our former glory echoing into a human experience.

In the year that king Uzziah died I saw also the Lord sitting upon a throne, high and lifted up, and his train filled the temple. Above it stood the seraphims: each one had six wings; with twain he covered his face, and with twain he covered his feet, and with twain he did fly. And one cried unto another, and said, Holy, holy, holy, is the LORD of hosts: the whole earth is full of his glory. And the posts of the door moved at the voice of him that cried, and the house was filled with smoke. Then said I, Woe is me! for I am undone; because I am a man of unclean lips, and I dwell in the midst of a people of unclean lips: for mine eyes have seen the King, the LORD of hosts. Then flew one of the seraphims unto me, having a live coal in his hand, which he had taken with the tongs from off the altar: And he laid it upon my mouth, and said, Lo, this hath touched thy lips; and thine iniquity is taken away, and thy sin purged. Also I heard the voice of the Lord, saying, whom shall I send, and who will go for us? Then said I, here am I; send me (Isaiah 6:1-8).

I used to see the above scripture as Isaiah being commissioned as a man here on Planet Earth in his generation, who could only be commissioned once his sin was removed through a burning coal. I always wondered how a burning coal could equate cleansing from sin, since only the blood of Christ can redeem us. Where is the hidden manna in this commissioning? Now I realize that Isaiah was encountering a memory of who he was and the reason he was sent in his generation.

If we are to make Jesus the example and heart of the Gospel, then we must find Him in the law and the prophets. We must also find us in Him in order to partner with being sent as Jesus was sent. Seeing the Lord high and lifted up can be seen two different ways: We can see Him as separate from us, or we can see that we were chosen in Him before the foundation of the world. I choose the latter perspective that declares we have always been a part of a multi-membered Body as spirit.

From this place we see Christ and His body seated above, and His train fills the temple. There is a lot of symbology we can glean from here that will unlock even more of our identity from a completed work. We are in Him in a seated rest, and we are the train of the many as one new man. We are also the seraphim speaking to one another, just as Malachi 3:16 says when we spoke one to another and a book of remembrance was written.

They spoke "holy, holy, holy" to one another about the nature of God. It was a horizontal proclamation, not a vertical one. Ephesians 5:19 reveals a parallel of how we as believers speak one to another in psalms, hymns, and spiritual songs. This was our identity in eternity! Be holy as I am holy! Our true identity is in the image of God as holy! Knowing the Father's affirmation and the way He sees us is key to us casting off the twisted image of being less than who we really are.

The "holy, holy, holy" proclamation, as though looking into the perfect law of liberty, then turns toward the earth proclaiming glory. The glory set before Jesus in Hebrews 12 is us. The glory Jesus had with the Father before the world is us. We are His glory, and when we see this face-to-face interaction of the image of God as holy within His body, then we will manifest who we were as holy in time. Being holy as spirit is glory in our human experience.

Elect according to the foreknowledge of God the Father, through sanctification of the Spirit, unto obedience and sprinkling of the blood of Jesus Christ: Grace unto you, and peace, be multiplied (1 Peter 1:2).

Our sanctification is in our origin and is seen as the foreknowledge of God. From this place obedience comes through grace and the Father does the works. My life in the blood begins to rain upon my human consciousness, renewing my mind in the Father's affirmation.

Isaiah is remembering from whence he came and the reason he was sent. His sin consciousness was of human understanding, for his mind could not reconcile all his human weaknesses with how the Father saw him before time began. And this is where the coal of fire comes as redemption. Symbolically, we are known as living stones in 1 Peter 2:5, built together as a holy temple. We are also described as being ministers of fire in Hebrews 1:7.

The Father was lifting the veil off of Isaiah by bringing to his remembrance who he was as spirit and the cry of Isaiah to a specific generation in which he would be sent. His humanity was struggling to receive this, so the Father sent his identity from eternity to kiss his human experience as a lively stone set ablaze with the love of God. We were in the seraphim interacting in the intentions of God. The fruit of this holy conversation was a manifest body seated in a seventh-day rest. All the echoes of every generation filled that temple as a train. Isaiah was seeing who he was in the multi-membered Body and his own participation and agreement to be sent in his generation.

Now of course, we experience our commissioning on Earth as it is in Heaven. Unfortunately, we reduce our calling to a time in our human life, thus judging by outward appearance something that we think we are now obtaining for the first time. This will only promote the need to measure up. Wherever I feel the need to measure up, I will eventually compete with and compare myself to others. These vain imaginations always try to exalt themselves above the experiential and eternal knowledge of God that has been hidden within us. We have our human view from Earth to Heaven, but we also have the eyes of the Spirit that see the end from the beginning. When we put our minds above, we get a clearer image that causes strife to cease. Rather than obtaining, we unveil the mystery of Christ.

Happy is the man that findeth wisdom, and the man that getteth understanding (Proverbs 3:13).

In my final depiction of who we were before time began, we will examine Wisdom who built her house and her sister, Understanding. Of course, there are many layers of application to this revelation, but we will focus upon identity, intention, and origin as the heart of the matter.

Solomon was given more wisdom than any other king. He was also given divine insight into building a temple that was the type and shadow of that which is eternal in the heavens. On the surface, Wisdom is known as a woman in Proverbs, yet scripture tells us there is neither male nor female, but all are one in Christ (Galatians3:28). We must look beyond human form and into the singularity of the Spirit. The masculinity and femininity of God is seen in Isaiah 11 as the seven Spirits of God.

Seeing that Wisdom is more than being intelligent in our minds and is, in fact, who God is will help us to see the reflections of who we are in Him. Everything God has, He is, which also reveals that everything we have in Christ is who we are. Taking this approach will remove much of the striving to obtain from God. What happens when I reach for what God has but I do not feel I have attained it? I will fall into confusion and self-evaluation, questioning whether the Lord wants to bless me. But if God is all He has and I am in Him, then I can simply embrace who He is to manifest what He has. This is the revelation of being complete and lacking nothing. From this place we will now see who we were in Wisdom and the parallel echo of the unseen into the seen.

But unto them which are called, both Jews and Greeks, Christ the power of God, and the wisdom of God (1 Corinthians 1:24).

So we know that Christ is the wisdom of God. He operated in the seven Spirits of God as a man in order to discern and walk in the purpose for which He was sent. We also see in Ephesians 3:9-11 that we as the Church will manifest the manifold wisdom of God.

And to make all men see what is the fellowship of the mystery, which from the beginning of the world hath been hid in God, who created all things by Jesus Christ: To the intent that now unto the principalities and powers in heavenly places might be known by the church the manifold wisdom of God, According to the eternal purpose which he purposed in Christ Jesus our Lord (Ephesians 3:9-11).

This manifold wisdom is a mystery we have been fellowshipping with that goes beyond time, taking us back to the beginning. There is an eternal purpose and intention hidden within Wisdom as the femininity of God. Part of who we are as spirit is hidden in this parable of Wisdom building a house. Let us look at a few more scriptures.

Length of days is in her right hand, and in her left-hand riches and honor. Her ways are ways of pleasantness, and all her paths are peace. She is a tree of life to them that lay hold upon her: and happy is everyone that retaineth her. The LORD by wisdom hath founded the earth; by understanding hath he established the heavens. By his knowledge, the depths are broken up, and the clouds drop down the dew (Proverbs 3:16-20).

Having length of days in one hand and riches and honor in the other speaks of a timeline human experience that is being prepared in which riches and honor will be a part of this unveiling. Ephesians 1:18 speaks of riches, glory, and inheritance hidden within one another. The word "glory" is also translated "honor." Can you see the parallel between what we were building before time to manifest it in time? We will also see that all her ways are pleasantness, and her paths are peace. This part is hard for us as humans to understand since we focus more on what is wrong than what is right. Let's look at a scripture to help us out.

And the peace of God, which passeth all understanding, shall keep your hearts and minds through Christ Jesus (Philippians 4:7).

This peace is in the pathway of the mind in which we discern good and evil. We will cover this in detail in a later chapter but let me give you just a sample that will tie this together for you. Our need to understand what has yet to be revealed exposes the intentions behind the pursuit of truth. It seems our hard path is needed to come to the end of our carnal understanding in order to remember the path of Father's intention in Wisdom, who built a house. This is where revelation flows freely in the peaceable path of remembering what we already built.

Have you ever battled belief systems in your own mind over and over again? Trying every known method of man to deliver yourself? It seems when we finally throw in the towel, we get hindsight into the real reason we walked through that dark season. All of a sudden, we are free and didn't know how we got there. This is known as reconciliation of that which was in Heaven to that which is on Earth (Ephesians1:10). Who you were in a completed work invaded what you had settled for in the lie of lack. We can also call this an echo.

Doth not wisdom cry? and understanding put forth her voice? (Proverbs 8:1).

Wisdom cries out to the simple-minded what was proclaimed as the Everlasting Gospel before time echoed at the appointed time into your human experience. The Gospel was already preached; we are simply remembering it. Only when our earthly wisdom has been exhausted will we begin to hear Wisdom speak.

What did Wisdom use to build her house? She used wood from a tree. She is a tree of life to those who lay hold of her. The Tree of Life is the family tree in which we as Wisdom built a future human experience. This is why we see that Wisdom founded the earth and Understanding founded the heavens. In all our getting, we must get Understanding. For Understanding carries holy intentions as to the purpose of redemption even before the beginning.

I could write an entire book based upon Wisdom who built her house, and maybe in the future I will. I do not want to exhaust this former version of you in this chapter but give just enough for you to enter into your own encounter of what has been built. Psalm 127:1 tells us that unless the Lord builds the house, we will labor in vain. To build the house before time ensures that what God decreed as authored and finished is not in vain.

Then I was by him, as one brought up with him: and I was daily his delight, rejoicing always before him; Rejoicing in the habitable part of his earth; and my delights were with the sons of men (Proverbs 8:30-31).

Wisdom built the future human experience from the heart of Understanding that carried Heaven's purpose. We as Understanding went from glory to glory in His delight. We were rejoicing in this future glory known as humanity. Our delight was in the sons of men before man was on the earth.

Proverbs 8:36 says, "But he that sinneth against me wrongeth his own soul: all they that hate me love death."

The carnal mind is death! Not a natural death, but the death of who we really are. When we make our humanity the foundation of our existence, we sin against our own soul. We choose the physical world as our reality over the Kingdom that is within us. To be renewed in the spirit of our minds is to remember we labored to enter the rest by building a house that was complete in Christ.

In conclusion of this chapter, I want to give some parallels of what we built as Wisdom and how we remember this in our humanity.

Wisdom hath builded her house, she hath hewn out her seven pillars: She hath killed her beasts; she hath mingled her wine; she hath also furnished her table.

She hath sent forth her maidens: she crieth upon the highest places of the city, Whoso is simple, let him turn in hither: as for him that wanteth understanding, she saith to him, Come, eat of my bread, and drink of the wine which I have mingled (Proverbs 9:1-5).

There are seven parallels or echoes in the above passage that will help us to partner with grace to unveil what is already complete.

The Seven Pillars

Seven is the number of completion and perfection. Revelation 3:12 tells us that he who overcomes shall be a pillar in the house of God. This represents the victory that is already yours. The renewed mind is hidden within these pillars. In other words, you are not trying to renew your mind, but unveil a renewed mind through the memory of your history in the intentions of divinity.

She has killed her Beasts ...

Everything you battle in your human journey has already been killed! Revelation 12:11 tells us that we overcame by the blood of the Lamb, the word of our testimony, and that we loved not our lives to the point of death. This scripture, which we will go into detail with later, is a pre-time battle that is connected with all the generations in the day they manifested. This is Wisdom building the house. Paul said it this way: Death works in us, but life in you (2

Corinthians 4:12). What appears to be destructive in our lives is only there to confront the carnal mind that projects death. Once the mind shifts into remembrance, victory is realized. This is where we loved not our (future human) lives to the point of death, because our intention for being sent was to lay down our lives for those we were sent to. The ability to relate to one another here is because we walked in one anothers' shoes. Being touched by the infirmities of others causes virtue to come forth as healing (Hebrews 4:15).

Mingling her wine ...

1 Corinthians12:13 tells us that we have all been made to drink of the same Spirit. Wine is depicted as communion and is the blood of Christ. Blood carries DNA or memory of what has been inherited within the family. It is one thing to walk through the shadow of death for others, but to be able to communicate life in

such a way that it releases the true identity of another is found in the mingling of every part doing its share. Relatability comes when I can speak your language. To look beyond the faults and failures of our human frailty and to see the potential of God in each other is the wine we mingled before the foundation of the world. Everything we built as Wisdom entwines with relationship with the brethren.

A furnished table ...

When I have realized that the beasts sent to destroy me could only rip open the book of remembrance, I will know how loved I am of my Father. Because I have received love, I can now give love. So I express this love by the mingled wine which invites my divine connections to the table. All those called to walk with me to fulfill my calling in the earth come to the table. This is where deep calls unto deep and we are fitly framed together as a habitation of the Lord (Ephesians 2:22). The flip side of this community is seen in iron sharpening iron, where we learn to fit together through a journey of contradictions. While my previous process of killing my beasts brought me to those I was sent to, I must now go even deeper into the enemy of my own mind. Colossians 1:21 tells us that we were enemies in our own minds. Psalm 23 tells us that our table is set in the presence of our enemies. No matter how much we think we know, the proof is in the interaction with people that are opposite of your personality. It is here that the feast exposes what is in our own minds that is still an enemy of what Wisdom built. Diversity is the foundation of unity!

Sending forth maidens ...

Even though we are all one in eternity, we will not be sent to everyone in our timeline human experience. Therefore, we exchanged scrolls, keys, and covenants with those who would be our closest friends on Planet Earth. You will know them instantly when you meet them here. Something breaks open inside you and there is an increase of everything you carry in the Spirit. These are the maidens who unlock you. For what we entrusted to one another before time, we sent into time as an inheritance in the saints. Revelation flows freely with your maidens, and all the prophetic flow they placed in you as Wisdom builds it.

The Cry in The High Places

As we see the other five parallels unfolding, we can now understand many of the different seasons in our lives that now seem to come together, proclaiming a theme. This is the sound of revelation in the high places. This is where all our divine connections, interactions, and feasting together begins to unlock the purposes of God in the journey.

It seems many of us started this journey with what we were called to do for God. But as the theme unfolds, we realize it had nothing to do with what we could do but who we are in Him— The cry of the culmination that brings destiny into identity, centering the heart or intention of God in the unified body of Christ. This is the place of knowing the ways of God. We walk through many seasons of expression that lead to maturity. And when maturity comes, we see the promises of God fulfilled. When Wisdom cries from the high places of the city, your humanity realizes eternity. You are no longer looking in a mirror dimly but face to face. You begin to know as you have been known.

The bread and wine mingled ...

This feast of bread and wine is different from all the feasting and drinking we have already experienced, mingled together in everything expressed and walked through in our human experience. This is the Body and the Blood of Christ. It is different from what we have been taught in modern-day evangelicalism. We are bone of His bone and flesh of His flesh. As the Body of Christ walks through the eating and drinking of Christ in one another, then the "us" and "them" mindset will be changed into an "us and we" mentality. We are to eat of this bread and drink of this cup till the Lord returns. We show this death till He comes.

The world is looking for something real, something genuine. Are we ready to give it to them? Showing the Lord's death till He comes is demonstrated in laying down our lives for one another. The degree to which we see our past brokenness as a present platform of grace is the same degree to which we can be vulnerable with one another. When the many believe they are the one, then we see the coming of Christ through His body.

Till we all come in the unity of the faith, and of the knowledge of the Son of God, unto a perfect man, unto the measure of the stature of the fulness of Christ (Ephesians 4:13).

The Everlasting Gospel is about unity in a journey that has no beginning or end. We were sent here to unlock truth from godliness in a world of contradictions that would prove godliness was truth. We are now remembering this journey on Earth as it is in Heaven. We have always been a household of faith, and the knowledge of the testimony of God will unveil this perfect plan in which we will finally realize everything God made was good!

Chapter Four

Sonship as a Body

For the earnest expectation of the creature waiteth for the manifestation of the sons of God (Romans 8:19).

In this chapter I will again reflect the mirror of who we were into who we are as sons of God. Since there is neither male nor female, I will use the term "sonship" to include both. While we have been taught that sonship is an individual "me and God" relationship, the heart of sonship is the multi-membered body known as the household of faith.

Through the generations, we have been slowly unveiling different aspects of sonship. Most of the definitions have been generic and impersonal, causing the hearers to try to obtain favor with the Father rather than to simply unveil it. We want to get to the heart of sonship, which begins with the Father's intentions.

We will begin with the only begotten Son of God as the centerpiece of sonship. But first, we must remove the conclusion that the Son of God was only an individual. Yes, He came as a man, but from whence did He come? He came from Heaven, from before the foundation of the world in which we were chosen in Him (Ephesians 1:4). All through scripture we see the many as one—from the remnant of Israel representing all of Israel to the seeds of Abraham being the seed which is Christ (Galatians 3:16).

Romans 8:19 reveals that all creation awaits the manifest sons of God. We see that what has been hidden in creation carries the expression of sonship. Sonship is not created; it is encoded within creation already. In John 1:4 we are in Him as light and life from the beginning. And if you understood the second chapter on Origin, you would understand that the beginning is not based in linear time, but a finished work now emerging into visibility. Realizing this truth will open up who you are in Him within the scriptures.

For whom he did foreknow, he also did predestinate to be conformed to the image of his Son, that he might be the firstborn among many brethren (Romans 8:29).

Not only were we foreknown in the Son, but He is the firstborn among the brethren. The word "among" also means "from within." To realize Jesus is the firstborn from within the brethren confirms that He was also made a priest according to the order (of the many) of Melchizedek (Hebrews 6:20). We can see that the One who came for the many is also One that came *from* the many. The natural reflects the spiritual; the seen reveals intentions hidden in the unseen. In the Gospel of Matthew, we see the genealogy of Jesus Christ presented. Just as the natural brought forth the firstborn from within the brethren, so it is in the spirit. Us chosen in Him before the foundation of the world would bring forth the only begotten Son of God.

As we begin to grasp our oneness in Christ, our struggle as victims of circumstance fades into the reality of being co-laborers in Him. What if the many from eternity sent the One into time? Since the Gospel was first preached to Abraham, let us gaze into this mystery and see the many as the One. In Genesis 15:5 Abraham is told to count the stars and the grains of sand in order to see his descendants. In Daniel 12:3, we are described as the stars of heaven. This is a beautiful picture of what it means to be surrounded with the cloud of witnesses described in Hebrews 12:1.

In Hebrews 11:10, we see that Abraham is looking for the city that had foundations made by God. Abraham is known as the father of faith because he had eyes to see beyond the natural and into the spirit.

But now they desire a better country, that is, a heavenly: wherefore God is not ashamed to be called their God: for he hath prepared for them a city (Hebrews 11:16).

This city with eternal foundations that Abraham was searching for was the household of faith. This household is the same house that Wisdom built. It is the seventh-day finished work in which all generations have been sanctified and sealed till the day of redemption. How did Abraham stand in faith and not stumble in unbelief?

He staggered not at the promise of God through unbelief; but was strong in faith, giving glory to God (Romans 4:20).

Our individual faith is only as strong as our unity in the household of faith. Romans 14 is all about the way we receive one another in the faith. Verse 23 tells us that whatever is not of faith is sin. Abraham saw the body of Christ in the stars and he saw the future human experience in the sand. He was carrying the One, the incorruptible Seed in the midst of the many from Heaven to Earth. He heard the Gospel and realized he was surrounded with such a cloud of witnesses that he drew upon the faith of many in the One in order to endure the journey. Abraham embodied the Gospel, journeying through the seen realm from an eternal perspective of the generational body of Christ. He acted out what Jesus Himself would walk through in His earthly ministry by offering Isaac on an altar. He knew that God could raise his son from the dead.

In the same way that Abraham walked out the eternal inheritance, so did Jesus. He came from above with His brethren in Him as light and life. His own blood carried the cry of Wisdom speaking to the mind of man. Jesus only did what He saw the Father doing, and what the Father was doing came from what Wisdom had built.

Let me balance this so as not to bring confusion. Jesus is the Head and we are the Body. I in no way want to reduce anything Jesus did in His human experience. Yet, Jesus has been exalted by the mind of man from a wrong perspective. We see Him as perfect but ourselves as separate from Him, thus becoming victims trying to attain perfection, or at least goodness. Exalting Jesus from a victim mentality is idolatry and must be dealt with in order for us to walk as Christ walked. Walking by faith through grace is how Jesus walked and carried Himself as a Son. This is the example in which we are to walk—not as separate from Him but being *in* Him. No man has ever walked like Jesus in the fullness of grace. Yet we are told, "greater things than these shall you do" (John 14:12).

What does it mean to walk as Jesus walked? First we must understand why He was sent. John 3:16 reveals that it was for love that He was sent. But I do believe we must untwist some perceptions that we have been taught. When we think about the Fall of mankind in the Garden of Eden as well as separation from God, are we seeing it correctly? Since God so loved the world, why would He first condemn it? Jesus is the revelation of the Father and God never changes. When we use Jesus as the measuring rod of the integrity of God, it seems to contradict God's nature when Adam and Eve sinned.

Could it be that we are basing redemption upon how Adam and Eve saw it rather than how the Father saw it? What if separation from God was how Adam and Eve viewed their lives through a tree of knowledge? Colossians 1:21 states: "That you were alienated and enemies in your minds by wicked works, yet now hath He reconciled." Could my separation be a perception and not a reality? Being "now" reconciled does not have a calendar date upon it; "now" is a present place outside of time.

The tree of knowledge is what much of the church has been looking through in order to be saved. We have been taught that we were separated in the garden and remain so until we come to the cross—but what if Christ came to awaken us to the reality that we were never truly separated at all?

Of which salvation the prophets have inquired and searched diligently, who prophesied of the grace that should come unto you: Searching what, or what manner of time the Spirit of Christ which was in them did signify, when it testified beforehand the sufferings of Christ, and the glory that should follow (1 Peter 1:10-11).

The prophets were prophesying things to come, yet the Spirit of Christ was already in them while they spoke. Some in the Old Testament caught the eternal revelation—men like Enoch, Moses, and Elijah. Enoch translated into Heaven before Jesus physically came to Earth to die on the cross. How did he bypass this and enter redemption before the time? He test-drove redemption from the foundation of the world.

And it was given unto him to make war with the saints, and to overcome them: and power was given him over all kindreds, and tongues, and nations. And all that dwell upon the earth shall worship him, whose names are not written in the book of life of the Lamb slain from the foundation of the world. If any man have an ear, let him hear. He that leadeth into captivity shall go into captivity: he that killeth with the sword must be killed with the sword. Here is the patience and the faith of the saints (Revelation 13:7-10).

Who was given the right to make war with the saints? Ultimately, it happened at the Tree of Knowledge. And from this tree came forth distorted imagery within the ego of man. We battle within our own minds—and when we settle for our humanity as the foundation of our existence, we reduce the image of God to only a human understanding. Living from a timeline perspective is where the enemy of our minds makes war with our true identity. In this place I believe I am separated, and my name is unknown to me in this place; therefore my name is not in the life of the Lamb. Yet, the scriptures declare: "The Lamb slain from the foundation of the world!"

This is a mystery, since it is outside of time and space—The foreknowledge of the Father that cannot have a pre-thought, since He is all knowing. And what is known in the mind of God is fully complete and lived out before it even manifests. Enoch translated because he test-drove redemption in the Lamb slain from the foundation of the world. It was done before it was revealed two thousand years ago. That which is seen comes from the unseen and the temporal from the eternal (2 Corinthians.4:18). But in the timeline, it is reversed, first in the natural and then in the spiritual (1 Corinthians15:46). The spiritual did not just happen for the first time after the physical; it was hidden within— like a mystery hidden from the beginning but manifesting at the appointed time.

We have this reversal not to attain redemption, but to unveil it. The first is last and the last is first; this is why God commanded the end from the beginning.

Jesus was sent from within the brethren that had already overcome by the blood of the Lamb! In Revelation 1:8 we see the God who was, is, and is to come. This proclamation sets the stage for the whole book of Revelation. Hidden within the Revelation of John is who God was before time, in time, and after time.

The angel sent to John to signify these things gives us a posture in which to understand the scriptures here. The word "signify" means "symbolize.". In other words, we are not to read this as literal but as a parable. There were current events happening in the day that John wrote the book of Revelation. These were relevant to the events of AD 70 and the destruction of the temple. There also are foundations of heavenly things symbolically being proclaimed to encourage the seven churches that were in tribulation at the time. Let us look at a particular passage of scripture that has been misunderstood by many but carries keys for us to enter the rest of God.

And there was war in heaven: Michael and his angels fought against the dragon; and the dragon fought and his angels and prevailed not; neither was their place found any more in heaven. And the great dragon was cast out, that old serpent, called the Devil, and Satan, which deceiveth the whole world: he was cast out into the earth, and his angels were cast out with him. And I heard a loud voice saying in heaven, Now is come salvation, and strength, and the kingdom of our God, and the power of his Christ: for the accuser of our brethren is cast down, which accused them before our

God day and night. And they overcame him by the blood of the Lamb, and by the word of their testimony; and they loved not their lives unto the death (Revelation 12:7-11).

Some scholars place this scripture in the future as a battle that will actually happen in our day and time. That somehow a devil is going to take over. The problem with this view is how it affects redemption and the integrity of God. Much of the end-time gloom-and-doom teaching places the book of Revelation as a future book in which the devil takes over everything. This theory causes the finished work of redemption to crumble and is an affront to God. Another view that has been presented is that it is a pre-time battle between the devil and Michael and the angels that led up to Satan manifesting as a serpent in the Garden of Eden.

While I do believe it is a pre-time parable, we must understand that parables are not to be taken literally, but symbolically. What can we glean from this battle before time that fits within the theme of the scriptures?

We find that a third of the angels fell. When we fast-forward to the Garden of Eden and the man and woman eating of the Tree of Knowledge, we see it was their *minds* that fell. In 1 Thessalonians 5:23 we are told that we have three parts: body, soul, and spirit. (I do believe we are one, with three dimensions to that oneness, but for the sake of symbology let us realize that one-third of us fell in the garden.) Remember what I wrote in Chapter Two concerning angels being echoes of who we were in another form? Michael and his angels fought and prevailed, and the saints overcame.

We see two categories presented in this war: who we were before a seventh-day finished work in the form of angels desiring to gaze into salvation; and as saints overcoming.

There is a three-fold truth. Our overcoming is Wisdom building a house. Remember, Wisdom has hewn her seven pillars (Proverbs 9:1). In Revelation 3:12 we see that overcomers become a pillar in the house of God. Go back to Revelation 2:7 and we see that overcomers eat of the Tree of Life. When we connect all these symbolic dots, we realize that Wisdom is a tree of life to those who find her (Proverbs 3:18).

So when did we overcome? When Wisdom built her house! When we as Understanding took Father's intentions that were heavenly and ate Wisdom as a tree, we then took what we ate and built a future human experience that was fully complete.

The other side to this revelation is the unveiling of our victory within the timeline human experience. When we remember who we were, then the mystery hidden from the foundation is revealed.

Now what about Satan? In considering the reality of an all-powerful God, who is the only real power here, I cannot comprehend any kind of real battle. When it comes to a match between God and an angel—well, there is no match. Satan (which can also be translated as "satans" in a plural adjective form), simply means "deceived" or "deceiver." So if this is a parable and not a literal battle, what does it represent? Let us go back a few verses and look at it in context.

And there appeared a great wonder in heaven; a woman clothed with the sun, and the moon under her feet, and upon her head a crown of twelve stars: And she being with child cried, travailing in birth, and pained to be delivered. And there appeared another wonder in heaven; and behold a great red dragon, having seven heads and ten horns, and seven crowns upon his heads. And his tail drew the third part of the stars of heaven and did cast them to the earth: and the dragon stood before the woman, which was ready to be delivered, for to devour her child as soon as it was born. And she brought forth a man child, who was to rule all nations with a rod of iron: and her child was caught up unto God, and to his throne. And the woman fled into the wilderness, where she hath a place prepared of God, that they should feed her there a thousand two hundred and threescore days (Revelation 12:1-5).

Some scholars interpret this dragon with seven heads and ten horns as Rome. Nero Caesar was the persecutor of the church at the time John was writing the Book of Revelation. We must consider audience relevance here: The woman with the twelve stars on her head giving birth to a man-child has many layers of interpretation. We can see the Lamb slain from the foundation of the world here, known as the finished works of God in the beginning. Also, we see Jesus coming in the flesh through the lineage of Israel represented in the woman. Thirdly, we can see the manifest sons of God emerging as the one new man within the body of Christ. In this book, I am focusing on our origin or identity from eternity, so we will be focusing upon the Lamb slain from the foundation of the world.

So when I piece together who we were in Michael, what Wisdom built in the spiritual Christ before time, and how we walked through the unveiling of that victory in our human experience; I see the battle between law and grace. The devil represents the ego of man exalted through the tree of knowledge and reinforced through the law of sin and death (Romans 1:2). The whole Bible is based upon the theme of the Old Testament under the law and the New Testament under grace. Who we were gazed into a future human experience that would walk through darkness under the law but would emerge victorious in the grace of Christ. And the posture of partnership in this grace is through the revelation of origin; being sent as Jesus was sent.

All the other interpretations of Revelation 12 also have truths hidden within them. I am not here to prove or disprove doctrinal accuracy. I am writing this book to bring identity to the forefront, focusing upon intentions as the foundation of partnership with the Father. Which one will profit us more? The seen or the unseen? What has happened in history or the purpose for which we were sent?

Before going any further into our victory in the slain Lamb from the beginning, I want to connect the dots concerning perception through the Tree of Knowledge. James 3:15 tells us that earthly wisdom is demonic. Colossians1:21 states that we were enemies in our own minds. When Jesus rebukes Peter in Mark 8:33, He equates Satan with the mind of man. While the Tree of Knowledge is what blinded us from the truth, it was Golgotha, the place of the skull, that woke us up.

With the purified you show yourself pure; and with the crooked you make yourself seem torturous (Psalm 18:26).

Does God really transform Himself as a torturous, wrathful God? Or is that just the lens through which we see Him when we believe we are enemies and separated? One of the side effects of the natural realm being our only reality is that the carnal mind makes everything look like death. The Tree of Knowledge shifts our reality from where we are seated in Christ outside of time into lack, loss, and separation. This is why God looks angry and wrathful in the Old Testament, yet He is a loving Father seen through the eyes of Christ. When they ate of the tree, Adam and Eve became aware of themselves through a twisted image. I believe the church has adopted the same perception in the many teachings today on spiritual warfare.

When was the battle won? Before it ever began! Who is the Lamb slain from the foundation of the world? Did Jesus suffer twice? No, Jesus did not suffer twice. What Jesus did as a man had its origin in Heaven. On Earth as it is in Heaven! But we do not see Jesus named in Revelation 12 as the one overcoming.

And they overcame him by the blood of the Lamb, and by the word of their testimony; and they loved not their lives unto the death (Revelation 12:11).

How could they overcome by blood that had not yet been shed? Who are "they"? John 5:39 states: "Search the scriptures; for in them ye think ye have eternal life: and they are they which testify of me."

The testimony of Jesus is the Spirit of prophecy (Revelation 19:10). And the word of our testimony manifested prophecy in the form of a man. We are told that we are co-laborers with God (1 Corinthians 3:9, 2 Corinthians 6:1). We just concluded that our laboring began when we accepted Christ as our Savior.

Let us look deeper into the blood of the Lamb. Revelation 7:14 declares:

And I said unto him, Sir, thou knowest. And he said to me, these are they which came out of great tribulation, and have washed their robes, and made them white in the blood of the Lamb.

I will use an analogy to help us understand the difference between the blood of Christ before time and the blood He shed within time. The above scripture tells us that they washed their garments white in the blood.

Blood is red, so how can it be white? In our bodies, we have white blood cells and red blood cells. Our white blood cells carry our immunity while our red blood cells carry oxygen. -Spirit is also known as breath, and when Jesus breathed upon the disciples, they received the Holy Spirit. If the disciples came from Heaven, didn't they already have the Spirit? Jesus did tell them that the Kingdom of Heaven was within them. We are seeing here an "on Earth as it is in Heaven" echo— visible manifestation in conscious awareness of that which was from the beginning. Washing my garments white is my immunity as an ambassador sent from one territory into another. As an ambassador I have diplomatic immunity because I am representing another Kingdom. In my human experience I must be awakened to remember I was sent as Jesus was sent, using breath or oxygen to animate who I have always been in my humanity.

This then is the message which we have heard of him, and declare unto you, that God is light, and in him is no darkness at all. If we say that we have fellowship with him, and walk in darkness, we lie, and do not the truth: But if we walk in the light, as he is in the light, we have fellowship one with another, and the blood of Jesus Christ his Son cleanseth us from all sin (1 John 1:5-7).

What message did they hear? That God is light. When did they hear it? Verse 1 tells us "in the beginning." The blood of Jesus here equals light, which is God. John 1:4 tells us the we are light in Jesus from the beginning. Since the blood of Jesus speaks better things than Abel spoke, what is the blood saying? It speaks our identity from eternity in God. Our redemption through the cross of Christ two thousand years ago was not about bringing us from separation back into union. It was about awakening us to the reality that we were always in Him. Jesus came to exemplify Sonship as the first born from within the many.

We overcame by the light and life of God, the memories of our origin or testimony in Him. The DNA of the Father was speaking who we are. All things are held together by the power of His word, and that word was in the beginning. In John 1:9 every man is lit on his way into this world. Our victory is in a seventh day, which is also Wisdom who built her house.

The war in Heaven is just another picture of the same day in which all humanity has been sealed till the day of redemption. This redemption is an unveiling or awakening out of the slumber that the Tree of Knowledge produced.

The eternal version sounds like this: we overcame by our identity as the household of faith before time, by the word or memory of our testimony in the history of our journey into the beginning, known as the testimony of God (1 Corinthians 2:1). And we loved not our future humanity to the point of death.

I will save that last statement for the next chapter, in which we will understand our choice before time to be sent as Jesus was sent. Yes, we had a choice. And our choosing in eternity is our predestination manifested in the timeline. But before we close this chapter, I want to help bring clarity to how Jesus overcame as a man.

These things I have spoken unto you, that in me ye might have peace. In the world ye shall have tribulation: but be of good cheer; I have overcome the world (John 16:33).

How did we participate with Jesus overcoming the world as the Lamb slain from the foundation? 1 John 5:4 tells us that the victory that overcomes the world is our faith. While the body prepared a place before time, Christ the head came into time. But Christ had to take upon Himself the mindset of humanity that was blindfolded from the memory of eternity. He then walked out every twisted image in a now embrace of the Father's perspective. Being tempted in every way of man, He overcame by remembering the victory of our faith as being one. In John 17:5, Jesus reaches for the glory with the Father before time and fully remembers His identity as one body. In this same chapter He declares, "I am no longer in the world."

Every lie man had believed passed through Jesus's consciousness. And when those thoughts would pass through, He would bring them captive to the Father's perspective. His death on the cross broke open the renewed mind on Golgotha, the place of the skull.

Then answered Jesus and said unto them, Verily, verily, I say unto you, The Son can do nothing of himself, but what he seeth the Father do: for what things soever he doeth, these also doeth the Son likewise. For the Father loveth the Son, and sheweth him all things that himself doeth: and he will shew him greater works than these, that ye may marvel (John 5:19-20).

The works of the Father were already finished since the foundation of the world. We see those works manifesting in a present-tense place through the life of Jesus when He walked the Earth. I love the second half of this passage above: "For the Father loves the Son and shows Him all the He Himself is doing."

What was Jesus doing or seeing Himself doing in this love embrace with the Father? He was remembering Revelation 12, where we overcame as the Spiritual Christ. The love embrace with the Father reveals the gratitude of the Son in that the Father did not send His Son to overcome sin by His own effort, but through a finished work.

God did not just roll the dice when He sent us to Earth. The fall of man had nothing to do with Adam and Eve not listening to God. If that were true, then divinity had to come up with a Plan B because He wasn't divine enough to foresee mankind's will overthrowing God's purpose. It was all planned for a reason.

In the next chapter we will talk about the potential reasons we chose to come to Earth blindfolded. Oh, what beautiful fruit can emerge from such chaos! Why did we love not our lives to the point of death?

Chapter Five

Son of Man, Son of God

The Son of man came not to be ministered
unto, but to minister, and to give his life a
ransom for many. Matthew 20:28

We all have a purpose in our lives, a destiny
within us. But many today wander through the
wilderness of their own minds, void of
understanding destiny. As we have journeyed
together through the pages of this book, we
have gained understanding of who we were in
Christ before time began. No matter how
liberating it is to gaze into eternity, knowing we
helped to build a house and were sent as
Jesus was sent; we need to be able to apply
this truth in our human lives. Jesus as the son
of man is our bridge for eternity to walk into
time in which we partner with grace.

The son of man is the one we identify with in our weaknesses, temptations, and trials. So how did Jesus overcome as a man? Previously I spoke about being the multi-membered body of Christ from the beginning. How we were in Him, overcoming in the 7th day that would secure every generation. In other words, God packed our lunch before sending us to school. But how do I apply this here, as a human? How do I do it without human effort or the need to measure up? How can I count it all joy when I am walking through life situations that seem opposite to who God says I am?

I will start by finishing what I said in the previous chapter. In Revelation 12:11 we overcame! I left out one component in chapter four that I will share here, that we might expand in depth what it means to "love not our lives to the point of death." Again, this book is about intentions. And when we do not understand intentions, we will be blind to purpose. Not just in what we are called to do, but in who we are. The son of man came not to be ministered unto, but to minister and give His life. Just as Jesus was sent to lay down His life, so we loved not our future human experience to the point of death. Let us define death in a healthy way.

Colossians 3:1-4

If ye then be risen with Christ, seek those things which are above, where Christ sitteth on the right hand of God. Set your affection on things above, not on things on the earth. For ye are dead, and your life is hid with Christ in God. When Christ, who is our life, shall appear, then shall ye also appear with him in glory.

Don't misunderstand the above scripture because it begins with the word "if." We tend to put conditions on whether or not we are in Christ when we see that word. A more accurate way of saying it is: if you have realized or awakened to the reality of being risen with Christ, then seek those things that are above. What and where is above? You are above and have been seated in Him forever. But in the beginning we built a house, and we built it because there was a purpose to coming into visibility as humans. So in order to understand many of the contradictions in life we must look to origin and the intention for which we were sent. What do we see when we put our minds above? That we died before we were ever born.

This was not a death like we have defined it in our earthly lives, this was a death that increased life. It was love that sent Jesus as the son of man and it is love that sent Jesus in you! When Christ who is our life shall appear, then you will appear with Him in glory. In eternity, we were in Him and as Him. There was an us in eternity yet as the one in singularity. When we appear in Him, it is not a separate person from Him, it is diversity within His imagery, known as your personality. Who you were as Christ in a multi-membered body said yes, send me! Our human experience is not based upon individuality but upon diversity of one body.

Our life was hidden in Christ, in God! This is the mystery hidden from the foundation of the world, Christ in us, the hope of glory (Col.1:26-27). When Jesus came He demonstrated our sonship to show us who we are. This is really what baptism is about. It is about remembering our death in Him to manifest our life which is Him. The difference between us dying before time and death that is experienced in our humanity is simple. Jesus said, those who believe in Me shall never die (Jn.11:26). Then why do we die? The carnal mind is death (Rom.8:6). Understanding the mind of the Spirit and our origin in Him swallows up the carnal mind and death is no more. Enoch had this revelation and did not see death.

Jesus tasted death for everyone (Heb.2:9). Not only did He walk through every carnal thought of man, as a man, but we in the multi-membered body tasted death by becoming mankind. We loved not our future human lives to the point of death. Now what does this look like? Well, as we read in Colossians 3:4 that when He shall appear, we shall appear in glory. Romans 8:18-21 declares:

For I reckon that the sufferings of this present time are not worthy to be compared with the glory which shall be revealed in us. For the earnest expectation of the creature waiteth for the manifestation of the sons of God. For the creature was made subject to vanity, not willingly, but by reason of him who hath subjected the same in hope, Because the creature itself also shall be delivered from the bondage of corruption into the glorious liberty of the children of God.

I don't like using the word suffering, even though it is clear in the bible. But when we use that word, we tend to believe that suffering equates worthiness. That I need to prove I am worthy of love so God is going to make me suffer. Many believe this today and remain victims in their minds, rather than sons who are well pleasing to their Father. Suffering is only negative when we see it from the carnal mind. In the mind of the Spirit, it is glory. Romans is telling us that what we go through in life that seems to be a contradiction to who we truly are will unveil who we truly are. Being made subject to vanity, not willingly sounds like we didn't want to go that route. This is referring to the human ego that was twisted through the tree of knowledge. In eternity, we were willing to love not our lives to the point of death.

Notice the context here, the suffering and the glory is not focused on our individuality but on community. The glory revealed as us is emphasized here. I am not getting glory handed to me if I don't complain when all hell breaks loose. If I keep a smile on my face, God will reward me. That is wrong thinking when it comes to how our heavenly Father sees us. Would you put your child through hell to prove he or she was worthy of your love? Christ, who is your life, is emerging through the groaning. We were made subject to vanity because we said yes Lord, send me. Who you are as spirit is love. And when we actually see who we truly are in Him, we will stop questioning why we walk through seasons of pressure and pain. Sonship is hidden within the groaning of creation.

Matthew 10:39

He that findeth his life shall lose it: and he that loseth his life for my sake shall find it.

This is not about self-sacrifice or depriving yourself from being you in order to appease God. This is about you losing the self-condemned mistaken identity and awaking to the glory of being your Father's son in eternity before time. Paul gave us some clues that will help us understand why contradictions in life are connected to love.

2 Corinthians 4:11-12

For we which live are always delivered unto death for Jesus' sake, that the life also of Jesus might be made manifest in our mortal flesh. So then death worketh in us, but life in you.

Over and over Paul will make statements that connect personal loss to someone else's breakthrough. Don't be discouraged at my tribulation which is your glory (Eph.3:13). For the sake of the elect, you suffer these things (2 Tim.2:10). We tend to take personally everything we go through in life. We judge ourselves as failures, not able to measure up or look spiritual. Part of us needed to take it personal for a time because the ones you are sent to have taken it personal.

Part of our sonship is being sent as Jesus was sent. This is a selfless act that comes not to be ministered unto, but to give our lives for others.

While the tree of knowledge produces self-preservation to live my life for me, who we truly are came to walk out the life of others that they might awaken to their sonship. In eternity, we spoke often one to another and a book of remembrance was written (Mal.3:16). What we spoke was promises to one another that would eventually be remembered through the contradictions of our humanity. We exchanged our identities with one another that would later be known as the inheritance in the saints (Eph.1:18).

We are known as kings, sons, and priests. We were kings in Him before time began. In Ezekiel chapter 28 we see a parable of Satan being thrown down before kings. Satan here is likened unto a man, the king of Tyre. This is a parable of how man fell into a mistaken identity through the tree of knowledge. But it is seen through the eyes of us as kings before time began. We knew we were going to walk through this journey blindfolded. It was not an accident, it was destiny. Who we were as kings gazed into a mystery of sonship. We said yes and died to who we were by putting on the blindfold of ego. Our spirit was hidden in Christ, not tainted by the human experience. But in order for our minds to remove the blindfold of being our own enemies, we have to walk through the priesthood.

Hebrews 5:11-14

Of whom we have many things to say, and hard to be uttered, seeing ye are dull of hearing. For when for the time ye ought to be teachers, ye have need that one teach you again which be the first principles of the oracles of God; and are become such as have need of milk, and not of strong meat. For everyone that useth milk is unskillful in the word of righteousness: for he is a babe. But strong meat belongeth to them that are of full age, even those who by reason of use have their senses exercised to discern both good and evil.

The whole chapter of Hebrews 5 reveals the purpose of priesthood. We will look at the end of the chapter first to understand the beginning. Being dull of hearing is our blindfolded process in which we take everything personal in our lives to expose and extract belief systems that cling to a mistaken identity. We must understand what sin actually means. The word sin is singular and plural and points to a mistaken identity in its singular form. In its plurality, it is the behavior of one who has a wrong perception of who they are. This is why we are tempted. James 1:14 tells us that we are tempted when we are drawn away. Being drawn away from how the Father sees us causes us to believe the lie that we lack something. Therefore, we are constantly trying to attain what has always been ours but is hidden.

So, when we are dull of hearing, it is because we have not recognized the word of righteousness within us, which is how the

Father sees us as complete. This is the first oracles of God as teachers. A teacher goes way beyond a bible study behind the pulpit. It is discerning good and evil through the eyes of being His righteousness. When we can see the Father's perspective in everything we have deemed loss and lack, then we can discern. Our life becomes the teacher for others to come into their identity. Looking through the lens of the tree of knowledge of good and evil is not the same thing as discerning good and evil. Can you find God's purpose in what you previously concluded was evil? Can God use everything in your life for good?

While the Spirit came to convict of sin, we have forgotten the same Spirit convicts of righteousness. Where sin abounds, grace abounds even more (Romans 5:20). When we understand that we are not sin, but sin that dwells in us (Romans 7:20), we will stop sinning. What we focus on, we magnify and make it our reality. This does not negate being responsible in the way we present ourselves; it enables true identity to emerge. Since sin is a mistaken identity then grace is my true identity. When I am confronted in life with opposites to what I have hoped for, then the motive behind my pursuit presents itself. The struggle in life is due to me making sin my identity and when confrontation arises, I will know this by my response to resistance. Once the man of sin which is ego has been revealed, I will see the contrast of grace in the midst of it.

Maturity uses frailty as a platform for grace. This becomes the Gospel I preach to others. Ego deems weakness as unspiritual, yet weakness and brokenness is the bridge of relatability for Christ to bring reconciliation through us.

For every high priest taken from among men is ordained for men in things pertaining to God, that he may offer both gifts and sacrifices for sins: Who can have compassion on the ignorant, and on them that are out of the way;

for that he himself also is compassed with infirmity. And by reason hereof he ought, as for the people, so also for himself, to offer for sins. And no man taketh this honor unto himself, but he that is called of God, as was Aaron (Hebrews 5:1-4).

Here is the great mystery of why we said yes to a human experience that would be filled with contradictions and the appearance of loss. Because we were sent to lay our lives down for the brethren. This is known as an honor to be ordained for other people. What gives us the power of life for others is that we walked through their death first. This whole journey is being walked out through the mind. When we are enemies in our minds, then our lives look like death. Compassion that reaches out to one another must first be able to relate through bearing one another's burdens. We are not just bearing burdens in the present, what we hide of past failures out of shame is where we laid down our lives for the brethren. Once we understand that being surrounded with sins and infirmities has nothing to do with our identity, then shame breaks off! Where there is no shame or self-evaluation, my past now becomes the teacher of oracles.

This is the priestly journey from kingship that breaks open sonship. He that knew no sin became sin for us! You as spirit who did not know mistaken identity chose to die and step into a timeline in which you agreed to walk out the belief systems of the ones you would be sent to. Let us go a little further by looking at 2 Corinthians 3:2-3:

Ye are our epistle written in our hearts, known and read of all men: Forasmuch as ye are manifestly declared to be the epistle of Christ ministered by us, written not with ink, but with the Spirit of the living God; not in tables of stone, but in fleshy tables of the heart.

We are written on each other's hearts! And the only way we get to read our lives hidden in one another is if the Lion roars to break open what has been sealed. Near the end of 2 Corinthians 3:17-18:

Now the Lord is that Spirit: and where the Spirit of the Lord is, there is liberty. But we all, with open face beholding as in a glass the glory of the Lord, are changed into the same image from glory to glory, even as by the Spirit of the Lord.

It is amazing what happens on the inside of us when we can see where the Spirit of the Lord is. Can you see Him at work through your failures? Then liberty will be the result! Liberation is defined in the above scripture as an open face and clear imagery. No masks, no walls, and no hiding from one another.

When I can see my journey in you and yours in me, then I can go to another glory through your story, which is really my story. Why? Because we talked about it before time and a book was written in us. 2 Corinthians 4 continues to unfold this revelation of us choosing to be sent and knowing by the Spirit that we would lay down our lives.

Therefore seeing we have this ministry, as we have received mercy, we faint not; But have renounced the hidden things of dishonesty, not walking in craftiness, nor handling the word of God deceitfully; but by manifestation of the truth commending ourselves to every man's conscience in the sight of God (2 Corinthians 4:1-2).

Now I can see! And because I now see a unity that agreed to this life and the purpose of what I once thought was suffering but now realize is love, I can receive mercy. This is where all the religious dos and don'ts just fall off. I am no longer trying to do something to be something. No longer using the word of God deceitfully to try and control others or manipulate myself. Realize that there was no bible written when Paul said this. He was not referring to the scriptures, he was speaking of Christ in us and as us. I have renounced deception! I am now seeing the Father's intentions; therefore I can see the heart of my brother and sister as Christ and His righteousness. It is a beautiful thing for brethren to dwell in unity! Let us continue to look into 2 Corinthians 4.

But if our gospel be hid, it is hid to them that are lost: In whom the god of this world hath blinded the minds of them which believe not, lest the light of the glorious gospel of Christ, who is the image of God, should shine unto them. For we preach not ourselves, but Christ Jesus the Lord; and ourselves your servants for Jesus' sake. For God, who commanded the light to shine out of darkness, hath shined in our hearts, to give the light of the knowledge of the glory of God in the face of Jesus Christ (2 Corinthians 4:3-6).

I love how Paul calls it our Gospel! He isn't using some generic term, the Gospel, but personalizing it to our communion together. It is hidden to those who are lost. We can easily

misunderstand what the word "lost" means.
Since we are hidden in Christ as a mystery.
We must understand that being lost is simply
being hidden. Paul speaks of fellowshipping
with the mystery of Christ in Ephesians 3:9. I
want to show you the other side of the same
coin. Mysteries are not only heavenly visions
we are gazing into. It is also things in our lives
in which we cannot understand. When we are
in life struggles that seem to have no purpose
to them, can we fellowship with that mystery?
Or do we try to deliver ourselves out of what
has yet to be understood?

I believe that hidden inside every
misunderstanding is the clear image of Christ.
To preach not ourselves, but Christ and
ourselves being servants to one another is how
we posture ourselves to understand mysteries.
My life isn't about me, it's about you! And when
I believe I am complete in Christ I will no longer
live my life for me. We see that God
commanded light out of darkness. God is not

afraid of darkness! Darkness and light are the same to Him (Psalm139:12). He is not delivering you from darkness as though there was some other power at work. God is all powerful, all means all! He has used the platform of shadows for light to bring expression. The light of knowledge in the midst of mysteries that look like contradictions. Just like glory looks like suffering! It is all in the way we perceive who we are, who God is, and the purpose for which we were sent. Have you ever had your picture taken with the sun on your face? It is so bright you cannot really see your expression. So it is with the journey through the valley of the shadow of death. The shadows of death in your life experiences becomes the bridge of life to those you are sent to.

We no longer believe in regret, because we believe that everything the Father sent us to do, we will. Where there is no regret, there is no vain imagination. For regret is my conclusion that God was not there with me. But when I am still blind to the reality of all things working together for good, then my conclusion of the past will stand in my present to exalt itself against who I really am as a son. Yet, what seems to be my enemy within my own mind, is attempting to veil my true identity and purpose. Let us look at how Jesus postured Himself in the midst of contradictions.

Yet it pleased the LORD to bruise him; he hath put him to grief: when thou shalt make his soul an offering for sin, he shall see his seed, he shall prolong his days, and the pleasure of the LORD shall prosper in his hand (Isaiah 53:10).

First I need to debunk our modern-day conclusion of how this scripture has been taught. It didn't please God to see His Son suffer. To see it this way reveals we have yet to truly understand the nature of the Father and why He sent His Son. Christ did not come to appease a wrathful God. He came to reveal the Father and who you have always been in Him.

His death on the cross was foreknown. God knew how mistaken identity would treat the truth of who we are as sons. When we are not living in the truth of identity, we will feel threatened by those who are. Yet, God was pleased with what would come out of the bruising of His Son, redemption.

Jesus knew that everything that came against Him could only produce redemption. He received everything in His life as from the hand of God because He was secure in His relationship with the Father. Even when Judas betrayed Jesus, it only fulfilled what was previously written. How can love be proven? Through contradictions! Do we not build trust with one another through a journey that proves itself in devotion and commitment?

Greater love hath no man than this, that a man lay down his life for his friends (John 15:13).

Was Jesus always the word that was then made flesh? Yes! Therefore the intentions to come to Earth was to prove love through opposites. Jesus made this clear when He said, if you only love those who love you, why should you get credit for that? (Luke 6:32). I believe we came from pure love before we were sent as Jesus was sent. But pure love is just one side of love. To come into the blindfolded journey, carrying one another in us gives opportunity for us to lay down our lives for one another. This brings pure love to unconditional love! Put these two together and we have perfect love!

There is no fear in love; but perfect love casteth out fear: because fear hath torment. He that feareth is not made perfect in love (1 John 4:18).

As we realize how beautiful the Good News of the Kingdom really is, then we understand this journey with new eyes. If everything that happened to Jesus only fulfilled the purpose for which He was sent, then why do we fight and war to obtain? Because we have yet to realize we are in our Father's hand. I want to share with you a mystery of another aspect of what Wisdom built that will help us understand the need for both the son of man and son of God in our journey. We will walk through this pattern that Wisdom built as a safeguard for your identity to emerge. This is known as the discipline of the Lord.

Wherefore seeing we also are compassed about with so great a cloud of witnesses, let us lay aside every weight, and the sin which doth so easily beset us, and let us run with patience the race that is set before us, Looking unto Jesus the author and finisher of our faith; who for the joy that was set before him endured the cross, despising the shame, and is set down at the right hand of the throne of God. For consider him that endured such contradiction of sinners against himself, lest ye be wearied and faint in your minds (Hebrews 12:1-3).

Before we unlock the discipline of the Lord, let me lay a foundation of the verses of scripture that lead into discipline. We see the many in the cloud of witnesses. This is who we were before coming into a human experience. Then comes the journey of resistance, sin, and finally victory in the race set before us. It is set before us, because we are looking at the end from the beginning as spirit. The end of the matter is seeing the many as one. Looking unto Jesus in what has been authored and finished. This is the place where we realize rest and dominion in a seated place of glory. This is how we are to discern our lives, from this perspective of origin and completion.

But as we look at verse 3, we see how our minds become weary through the contradiction of sinners. Realize that this is not talking about judging others as sinners, but about how we judge ourselves through a sin consciousness. We get stuck in self-evaluation and condemnation which keeps us self-sabotaging our lives. This leads us into the discipline of the Lord. Before we look at more scripture about

God's discipline, I must ask a question. Does God discipline you as a reaction to your action here on Earth? Or does He already know what you're going to do before you do it? Many times we reduce God to a human response and think that God disciplining us is punishment for what we did wrong.

Because God is all- knowing, I believe Wisdom encoded the discipline of the Lord into your human journey. I call this being pre-disciplined. Let us look at another scripture!

Now faith is the substance of things hoped for, the evidence of things not seen. For by it the elders obtained a good report. Through faith we understand that the worlds were framed by the word of God, so that things which are seen were not made of things which do appear (Hebrews 11:1-3).

While we have been taught to have faith in our human experience, we are faith as substance. To have the faith of God is a biblical principle but few have understood it. When we only see what God has, we constantly are trying to obtain from a place of lack. But when we realize everything He has is who He is, we can simply embrace who He is and allow everything He has to flow forth. Because we are in Him and seated with all spiritual blessings, we can now see that faith as who we are in spirit must manifest as evidence in our humanity. The evidence of who we are as faith is known as the worlds framed with the word of God. Since there was no bible when this occurred we must realize that as living epistles of Christ, our human life would carry sonship hidden within it.

All creation is groaning and sonship groans within it. Everything in your life that continually resists you, is not really resisting you. It is resisting what you are not. We in Christ encoded into our lives contradictions that would fight against wrong perception. This is the safeguard to use all the groaning in our lives to manifest sonship in the midst of it.

Now no chastening for the present seemeth to be joyous, but grievous: nevertheless afterward it yieldeth the peaceable fruit of righteousness unto them which are exercised thereby. Wherefore lift up the hands which hang down, and the feeble knees; And make straight paths for your feet, lest that which is lame be turned out of the way; but let it rather be healed (Hebrews 12:11-13).

Once we begin to see the discipline of the Lord from a place of co-laboring in Christ, we will yield the peaceable fruit of righteousness. Peaceable fruit comes when the peace of God surpasses my own understanding, bringing my awareness into alignment with who I really am as a son of God. James 3:17-18 reveals the same fruit of righteousness and peace when we operate in heavenly wisdom. Heavenly wisdom begins with us realizing the house we built. This is where that which was broken and lame is healed and utilized as grace in our lives. We as humans are always trying to throw out the bad and get the good. Instead, we should embrace what shakes us to reveal within us a Kingdom that cannot be shaken. A lot of the doctrines we have learned concerning spiritual warfare and deliverance have been erected to fight against the discipline of the Lord. This is why the only fruit we see in our warfare is suspicion, competition and division.

Let us summarize what it means to manifest on Earth as it is in Heaven who we are as sons of men and sons of God. We said yes to be sent as Jesus was sent. We agreed to much of the contradictions in life before we ever came here. We encoded unconditional love and grace into the structure of our human experience, to use opposites in life to prove love. We carried each other through a blindfolded experience that would eventually awaken us to an inheritance within each other. This is where unity works! We are never told to get unity, only to keep unity (Ephesians4:3). Therefore we know no one after the flesh but after the Spirit (2 Corinthians5:16). Everything in our lives that has appeared to be weakness, loss and lack becomes the present platform of grace and glory when we realize nothing can be lost. Jesus Himself demonstrated total dependency on His Father because He understood that He came from Heaven and was sent because of love.

What a beautiful picture of redemption and purpose that enables us to walk as Christ walked, knowing we said yes because of love. I know this can be confusing when we are still struggling to defend ourselves as victims of circumstance. I said yes to all that pain and abuse I walked through? There are really only two ways of looking at this. God knows everything before it happens. So either He knew what you would walk through and it would have no purpose or we agreed because of purpose. I choose to believe we agreed to come to Earth and expand who we were into the proof of love manifested. We can always find what is wrong with our lives, and it has never added one bit of fruit. Or we can believe that our Daddy packed our lunch before sending us with a note inside that said, don't forget to share your lunch with your friends.

In Chapter Six, I will talk about the revelatory realm and the renewal of the mind.

Chapter Six

Spirit of Revelation

That the God of our Lord Jesus Christ, the Father of glory, may give unto you the spirit of wisdom and revelation in the knowledge of him: The eyes of your understanding being enlightened; that ye may know what is the hope of his calling, and what the riches of the glory of his inheritance in the saints, And what is the exceeding greatness of his power toward us who believe, according to the working of his mighty power (Ephesians 1:17-19).

The Spirit of revelation has been depicted as the Holy Spirit or one of the seven spirits of God mentioned in Isaiah 11. This has been taught as being separate from us, and therefore means we need to get something we did not previously have. Even the above passage appears to tell us that we must first receive it. But hopefully by now, you will understand that there is no separation because we were in Him before time began.

The Father wants you to know that everything you are as spirit has been freely given. Our struggle in trying to get revelation comes from the lie of lack and separation. But once we see that everything God has, He is, then we will realize we lack nothing because we are one with Him and in Him. Because we are one spirit, we are made of revelation. And though there are many different layers to getting revelation in our lives, the heart or foundation of the matter is that you *are* a revelation. You who were Wisdom who built a house remembers through being Revelation in your human experience.

No matter how much this is your reality as spirit, we need to have the eyes of our hearts opened. This is known as renewing the mind. The heart of your mind is the lens through which you see yourself. We as human beings tend to project outwardly what we truly believe.

Most people in the beginning of renewing the mind have no clue what they really believe about themselves. We just fly by the seat of our pants from one reaction to the next. We often draw our conclusions about who we are from other people's reactions to us and use those conclusions to define ourselves.

Before we jump into being revelation as a memory of who we have always been, let us first talk about how the mind works and reacts. We have two sides of the brain: the intellectual side and the creative or experiential side. On the surface, we try to safeguard ourselves through intellectual logic as proof of reality, but we actually live and respond from the emotional side of our past experiences. The mind works by association. In other words, our reactions are based upon where we have been before. This is why when a spouse or close friend says something to us that triggers us, we will react defensively.

What is a trigger? A trigger is a lie we have believed about ourselves or someone else. It is based on events in our lives when we have been victimized, betrayed, rejected, etc. Of course, we do not want to invalidate the pain of someone who has gone through a lot of trauma, but we also do not want to promote or feed the lies people have believed. There are facts and there is truth. The fact that someone rejected me doesn't have to define me as being "a reject." Yes, this person projected the lies they believed about themselves upon me. If I adopt that experience as truth, then I will live from a place of being self-protective, waiting for the next person to reject me. In fact, when we build our lives upon these twisted images, we will feel more secure around people who reject us than those who accept us.

Most of our triggers were formed in childhood. The formation of our character created lenses through which we would view the world for the rest of our lives. The way our parents and siblings treated us, or the way we perceived their treatment of us, will lead us to expect how we will be treated and loved by others.

There is good news! Triggers are bridges that enable you to reinterpret the past. If you can see it from the mind of Christ, you will realize that when you are triggered, it can be a reset button that restores the years the cankerworm has eaten.

Let me give you an example. My wife hates spiders. And, being the prankster I am, once put a rubber spider on her shoulder. She jumped and screamed! To her it was real, yet it was only a rubber spider. That's how lies work in our lives.

How many rubber spiders have you encountered that felt real at the time? We live from our experience, not our intellect. As Christians, we try to pile biblical information into our minds to drown out what we really believe about ourselves. Much of our striving to attain spirituality originates in self rejection and fear. I cannot renew my mind by studying scriptures. They may help me to see areas where my mind needs to be renewed, but it will usually be from the wrong lenses.

Here is where the rubber (spider) meets the road:

It is not what you believe but why you believe it that matters most. Getting to the reason *why* we pursue truth is the key to renewing the mind. We live in a dual world: what is complete as spirit runs parallel to what is unveiling or echoing into our human awareness. Since awareness is the key to a manifestation or reality that we experience, we must look at how we see ourselves first.

On Earth as it is in Heaven is what our parallel life is constantly reflecting. We are complete in Christ, seated together in heavenly places. And we are walking through life in the midst of contradictions to this reality. Our intentions come from eternity, but our reactions are seen in time. Let us look at what I call the "mirror effect" or "the fun house."

For if any be a hearer of the word, and not a doer, he is like unto a man beholding his natural face in a glass: For he beholdeth himself, and goeth his way, and straightway forgetteth what manner of man he was. But whoso looketh into the perfect law of liberty, and continueth therein, he being not a forgetful hearer, but a doer of the work, this man shall be blessed in his deed (James 1:23-25).

Our natural mind is conscious in the physical world; the subconscious or unconscious mind is where intentions are. When Adam and Eve ate of the tree of mistaken identity, they became aware of the natural. They lost sight of the Kingdom within them. Everything in their lives then became based upon *doing* something to *be* something.

Have you ever had one of those days when you felt depressed but had no clue why you felt that way? Everything externally was going well, but you felt terrible anyway. What do most people do in this situation? They distract themselves to feel better. They focus on something else or someone else to forget about what they feel. Most people do not even know what they feel or who they actually are in the midst of feeling. We conclude that one feeling is good and another is bad. What if emotion is neither positive nor negative? What if, at a subconscious level, we have a wrong conclusion about ourselves based on an event in the past? What if this conclusion is what is throwing us into the illusion of duality?

Scientists believe that we are only conscious of about 3 percent of our reality, a two-foot perspective in front of us. Imagine if you could only see one foot to the left and one foot to the right. We wouldn't really want to run and play in a carefree life, would we? We would be conscious of loss and would tread very carefully. Many are too afraid to actually live life because they cannot really see. So, 97 percent of our reactions are coming from the subconscious part of the mind. We react but we have no clue why.

Even though the subconscious can sabotage us through reaction, when it is renewed, it carries revelation as the memory of eternity from whence we came. Since Adam lived from the intentions of God before eating of the physical world as his reality, we can see that when revelation opens up, we discern purpose. This funhouse-mirror effect isn't always fun when we do not know how to posture ourselves in the midst of triggers. In order to heal the breach between the conscious and the unconscious, we need to awaken to the Kingdom within. How I do this is by realizing there is a purpose for everything in my life. And by looking at life this way, I can get a new perspective. I also look at everything and everyone as a mirror. We all do this, but most of the time we are looking at ourselves in others from a natural mind instead of the spiritual mind.

When I am projecting lies about myself onto others, I will reinforce those lies when others react harshly to what I am projecting. I will walk away not remembering who I was. When I take every confrontation as an opportunity for liberty, then I will utilize opposition to expose and remove lies.

We must be honest with ourselves if we are going to end the cycles of self-manipulation. I manipulate myself every time I see a reflection and blame the person mirroring it. Being a doer of the word by looking into the perfect law of liberty has nothing to do with doing something to be something. Jesus said, "I only do what I see My Father doing." This also means to be who my Father is.

For ye are yet carnal: for whereas there is among you envying, and strife, and divisions, are ye not carnal, and walk as men? (1 Corinthians 3:3).

Proverbs 23:7 tells us that as a man thinks, so is he. This does not mean he actually is what he thinks, but what he thinks has become his reality. We create our own reality by how we view ourselves. I can only love others as I love myself, so the key to loving myself is to see my weaknesses and failures from a different perspective. Jesus could only do what He saw the Father doing because the Father loved the Son and showed Him what He was doing within the Father before He was sent.

Everyone is a mirror in your life of either what you have believed or what your about to believe. We have those who irritate us and those who challenge us. We have people as road signs in our lives that we admire and want to be like. These represent you in the future. But when your view of yourself is skewed, jealousy will arise. This desire to compare did not just come upon you, it was surfaced through the people.

If we can understand that our present situation is not what is causing pain, but it is an echo of past conclusions, then we can escape the trap of blame. This is the fruit of the Tree of Knowledge, or as I call it, ego. "The woman gave me the fruit." "The devil made me do it!" We project outwardly to protect the lies we have believed.

I have been called the poster child of renewing the mind. I have had several bad relationships in which my own self-rejection and self-sabotage dictated who I was. When my wife and I were married, I knew that eventually I would destroy the relationship, as I always had before. I was always waiting for the other shoe to drop, constantly telling her that she should just move on because I wasn't good enough for her.

The first year of our marriage was tough. I did everything I could to get her to reject me. Of course, I was not conscious of doing this, and that is why triggers are lies. We never plan this out--it is simply a reaction from a wrong perception. But my wife just kept loving me until I finally saw the lies I had believed about myself. From that point on I began to see keys to having a healthy relationship that I want to pass on to you.

These keys have made my marriage maintenance-free! So here it is!

When your spouse triggers you, choose not to hold them accountable even if they are in the wrong. This sounds backwards, but remember, if you're triggered, then the motive is to correct another to protect the lies you believe about yourself. (This was a hard one for me since I am a communicator. I had to let go of my rebuttals.)

Secondly, you must realize that no matter what your spouse is doing to you, if you're triggered, then they are your deliverer. Proverbs 27:17 tells us that iron sharpens iron. Sparks are going to fly if you want to be sharp and cut through that ego. Make your pain about you and not your mate! When I started implementing this, everything changed. Every argument renewed my mind and brought deeper bonds with my wife. (Of course it is always better if you both agree to do this.)

Let's look at the flip side of the same truth. To understand whether you are the deliverer or the one being delivered will depend upon who is triggered. If you are not triggered and your spouse is, then you can hold your mate accountable. Now how do we do this?

First, let me share about two extremes. One extreme is to try to rescue your mate from the pain he or she is feeling. Don't do that! We have to walk through it in order to get the revelation of how bound we have been to that lie.

Have you ever been in a room that was pitch black, with no light whatsoever? Just a flicker of light would cause you to squint. All it takes is a tiny amount of light to show the contrast, and so it is with truth. We do not need some grandiose truth; we need to see a flicker of light in the midst of darkness.

The other extreme is to ignore it altogether. We think it's best not to rock the boat at all. But we do not need to have the answers; we simply help to direct our mate to respect their emotions by not stuffing them. Be available and be love! It is that simple!

Now if we can apply this to every relationship, we will experience peace and rest like never before. Most of the drama in our lives, we create. To receive everything as from the hand of God is to also believe that the Father has your best interest at heart. What if your life has been encoded from eternity to only resist everything that you are not, so that everything you are can fully manifest? Renewing the mind is not attaining the truth, it is unveiling it. Many veils will be ripped off for you to realize truth. Contradictions and oppositions become our best friends when we know we are secure in the Father.

There is a two-fold revelation in the midst of contradictions being used to unlock the real you. First, we can know experientially that God is who He says He is. We cannot know that God is faithful until we are faithless. Without our faults and failures, we will still base our acceptance upon our good works. Secondly, we realize we are walking this out for others. We are only relatable in the areas where we have walked in each other's shoes. This is the bridge of compassion that bears one another's burdens. Your journey is not about you, it is about everyone else. Jesus said, "I come not to be ministered unto but to minister and give my life a ransom for many" Matthew 20:28. If I do not believe I am complete in Christ, then I will argue against this truth. I will struggle to believe that others will do the same for me. We need to get past this lie.

Let us look at one more scripture on renewing the mind and some components that will help posture you to do it well.

I beseech you therefore, brethren, by the mercies of God, that ye present your bodies a living sacrifice, holy, acceptable unto God, which is your reasonable service. And be not conformed to this world: but be ye transformed by the renewing of your mind, that ye may prove what is that good, and acceptable, and perfect, will of God (Romans 12:1-2).

Renewing the mind is the automatic response to rightly seeing one another as assets in each other's lives. Romans 12 begins with the word "brethren"! Spending time alone with God and in the Word is great. You will ponder truths and get great revelations—but to live those revelations out, we need interactions with people. And only in the application of interaction is there proof of a renewed mind.

The posture of realizing mercy in the way we treat one another causes us to celebrate the heart of identity in the brethren. We begin to realize we are holy and acceptable and are able to freely lay down our lives for one another. Laying down your life begins with letting down the walls and being real with the people closest to you. This is the opposite of being conformed to this world! And when love has been proven through the journey together, you will realize you are accepted in His goodness, perfect and complete, lacking nothing.

We have to get beyond the fear of being deceived before we can be transparent with one another. Guess what? We are *all* deceived somewhere. We are constantly being unveiled in the truth of identity, and what is yet to be revealed feels like deception. But when we place false expectations on ourselves and others, then we must build walls of doctrines to protect ourselves from one another.

The Father sees you as accepted, as good, and as perfect in His eyes. When we can see His purpose in the midst of every opposite circumstance, then we can understand why we walked through the contradictions.

Now that we have established how the mind reacts and responds, as well as the need for mirrors, let us unlock the Spirit of Revelation.

Ultimately, revelation is your invitation into divine encounters. These encounters are actually memories of who you have always been before time began. Revelation is your spiritual territory that you walked in before you came to Earth. To manifest on Earth as you are in Heaven begins with remembrance. You are His opinion sent as dominion. Jesus said, "Take no thought for your life." That's because you are His thought sent into this life. Taking no thought has nothing to do with having a blank mind. It simply means to be neutral, without conclusion. We limit truth when we conclude. Since triggers are based on our earthly conclusion of our human history, when this flips over in the Father's perspective, we begin to remember our origins. Eternal memories are triggered through seeing the Father's perspective in our earthly contradictions.

Now when I begin to unveil revelation, I am usually introduced into destiny before identity unveils. Destiny is what I am *called to do*, while identity is *who I am*. Eventually these blend together as we mature, but in the beginning we are still driven to perform. This is why God will emphasize doing before being, because we have to first burn out of our own works to enter the rest of just being.

Secondary truths and revelations will eventually find themselves within the structure of the house that Wisdom built. When all the striving has ceased, we will see greater glory in the darkness than we previously did in the light. The theme of who we are will emerge, and the diverse expression of why we were sent in the first place will become clear. Destiny will become the looking glass for others to behold your communion in the Father. We will realize that light and darkness are the same to us, and the shadows are simply bringing the contrast to expression.

When I began to forerun this revelation of eternity over twenty years ago, it was very frustrating. I had all these glorious encounters and revelations but did not know how to implement them in my daily life. In fact, my life was a mess when it came to relationships lasting, and I had so many trust issues that I used my Bible knowledge to protect myself from people who are made in the image of God. Some believe that when Adam and Eve were hiding from God in the midst of the

Garden, they were actually hiding in the branches of the Tree of Life. Isn't it ironic to try to hide from God while being in Him? I think we can use our knowledge of God to try to hide from Him. Why do we isolate ourselves from one another? Because we are hiding from the parts of ourselves that are hidden within others.

What changed for me was seeing every contradiction in my life from a son's perspective instead of from a victim's. Let me illustrate this by using quantum physics.

The theory of quantum entanglement is that two atoms can be connected or entangled together. It does not matter whether they are one mile or a thousand light years apart—they will respond to one another. Their response is opposite to one another, yet precise. While one atom will spin clockwise, the other will spin counterclockwise. They do this exactly at the same time. So it is with us. We are walking through eternity as spirit, and we are walking out a human experience in time.

And no man hath ascended up to heaven, but he that came down from heaven, even the Son of man which is in heaven (John 3:13).

Jesus came from Heaven but was also in Heaven at the same time. Beauty for ashes, oil of joy for mourning, and the garment of praise for heaviness is not me obtaining but unveiling. I do not lack anything and therefore I do not need God to fix anything. I need to realize that being born from above is not about me going to Heaven when I die; it is the revelation and remembrance that I came from Heaven.

Beauty in the mind of the spirit looks like ashes to the carnal mind. I am simply shifting my perception from an earthly view to a heavenly one. We are entangled from Heaven to Earth, and every contradiction is what helps us remember. This is how we apply heavenly wisdom! Only when I understand how the

Father sees me in my brokenness will I be able to manifest the mysteries of eternity.

Another example of the contrast in the way in which we perceive is seen in the difference between the world and the earth. Jesus said, "In the world you have tribulation, but be of good cheer, I have overcome it." What did He overcome? Man's perception of His environment. Jesus overcame as a man in the same place physically that man could not overcome. He did not do it as God, but as a man. So why can't we do the same? Because we have missed the point of Jesus coming.

The earth is the LORD'S, and the fullness thereof; the world, and they that dwell therein (Psalm 24:1).

We are told the Earth belongs to God. That everything He made was good. Jesus told us that the meek shall inherit the earth. Isaiah had a vision of seraphim declaring glory that is already in all the earth. So where is it?

It is in you. The Kingdom is within! Adam and Eve became aware of the natural realm as their origin. When we are outwardly focused, we become entangled with the cares of this life. "The world" is a belief system where tribulation is constantly happening. It is the place of being tutored by the Law, of being attacked by demons, and the place of persecution. The world is the enemy, which is the carnal mind.

The earth is the Kingdom within you that lacks nothing. Everything works together for good; there is no battle because you have entered the place of rest. This is where the unity of the saints abides. It is known as the secret place of the Most High. It is a secret, hidden from the ego of man. As we go on to maturity we will stop repenting from dead works and start manifesting God's works. Eventually we will see the Kingdom within us come upon our human experience—shifting and changing the elements around us because we now see clearly. The supernatural that Jesus manifested was simply real life outside a worldly mindset.

Let us close this chapter with the opening scripture of Ephesians 1:17-19. Ephesians opens with who we are presently in Christ as spirit—where we came from in Christ from before the foundation of the world, and how everything God reconciles in our human experience is all from within Him. The proclamation is that there has never been separation! It is this reality that breaks open the Spirit of Wisdom and Revelation—who you were and who you are in the Father of Glory. You are His glory and He is the Father of all the glories you have walked through from eternity into time. And in this foundation of faith as the household of faith, we realize the hope of His calling. It is also our calling that we all agreed upon. When we see Him, we will be like Him! We are simply opening our eyes to the reality of unity and what was entrusted to one another before time that is manifesting as inheritance within time.

All that we journey through together unlocks the reality of the grace and faithfulness of God. And this grace is transferable in and through one another as we realize we have always been one!

If ye have heard of the dispensation of the grace of God which is given me to you-ward. How that by revelation he made known unto me the mystery; (as I wrote afore in few words, Whereby, when ye read, ye may understand my knowledge in the mystery of Christ) Which in other ages was not made known unto the sons of men, as it is now revealed unto his holy apostles and prophets by the Spirit (Ephesians 3:2-5).

Chapter Seven

The Quantum Quo

So then faith comes by hearing, and hearing by the word of God (Romans 10:17).

In this chapter we will use quantum mechanics to help you understand from another angle the concepts of eternity and time. Don't worry; I will not be going into equations or the mathematics of quantum, which can be boring! Instead, I want to give you some parallels that will hopefully break more boxes off your thinking and open more doors of experience for you to enter who you are as spirit.

Quantum Faith

Quantum faith is the whole body of Christ as one in the unseen realm before the beginning.

Who you were then slowed down to sound as you heard the Gospel (Colossians1:23). You are a living epistle, the Word with God in John What was heard was also built as Wisdom's house, known as the seventh day.

In quantum physics, everything has frequency and vibration. You, your children, your car, and even the furniture you sit on. You can't see it because it is too small to see from a human perspective. If you could, it would be vibrating, thinking and living (2 Corinthians 4:18). In our human understanding faith comes to us and we hear with reason and intellect through studying the Bible. But in the quantum realm, you were faith that heard a sound of a future version of you that is known as a living epistle or human experience.

Our finite mind is like a fly on the wall of an infinite world that is listening to every conversation of ourselves in a multiverse. This can blow our minds—and that is exactly what we need to break out of a worldly perception.

Quantum physics is like the encoding within a computer program; us in Christ is the programmer that is building a virtual-reality human experience. In the finite, the naked eye sees the graphics or charts that relate to what is familiar to us in a three-dimensional world. But underneath the surface, it is seen in codes. Remember the movie *The Matrix*? It is exactly like that. Seeing what is behind the hologram is seeing in the spirit (or in the parlance of our analogy, it's like taking the red pill Morpheus offers Neo).

This is why we get entangled with the cares of this life: because we are not seeing truth or purpose hidden within it. The encoding of who you are as spirit is made up of frequencies that produce energy echoing into visible form. What you believe produces energy and atmosphere!

Have you ever noticed that when you're angry, others get upset with you? Nothing seems to go right when we are upset. But when we are full of love, people are drawn to us, they honor us, and everything falls into place. It is easy to fall into the trap of believing the outward visible world is a threat to who we are in the spirit. But what is actually happening is that we are creating the environment around us by the way we think. As a man thinks, so is he (Proverbs 23:7).

Intention is the sound of creation. When we operate at lower frequencies or carnal thinking, we create warfare for the mind. The natural world around us is the product or fruit of the sound we carry. Love is the highest frequency that bridges eternity into time. This is where miracles happen, and forgiveness and reconciliation take place.

The law of nature, like gravity, is what most of us are conscious of. What goes up must come down! But once you become conscious of the quantum realm, you will realize nothing is there till you look and are conscious of it. Our awareness creates the reality of it in our lives.

Scientists have discovered that the electron that orbits the nucleus is not always there in particle form. It exists like a wave or cloud that is everywhere at the same time. Yet, when it is observed or looked at, it changes to appear as a dot or particle. So what has been witnessed changes form after it is seen. We as faith behold what is revealed, and in the beholding, that creative frequency unfolds through us. We are waking up to the truth through observation. Observation has no conclusion but is neutral in order to see beyond the boundaries of conclusion (John17:16).

Faith observes that which is not, or that which is not of human conclusion (Hebrews11:1-3). In quantum mechanics, observation changes it. You are really not sure if it existed until it is observed. I believe our memories as spirit before time can be observed in our human experience. This is known as signs, miracles, and wonders and contradictions. As your faith is, so be it unto you (Matthew 9:29). Faith is a memory of who you were that is being remembered in a human experience. The worlds were framed with the Word of God, which is your identity from eternity. This is where all creation groans to unveil your sonship.

"We are slowed-down sound and light waves, a walking bundle of frequencies tuned into the cosmos. We are souls dressed up in sacred biochemical garments and our bodies are the instruments through which our souls play their music."

~ Albert Einstein

In reading this quote from Albert Einstein, I realize that we as humans tend to compartmentalize our life into three parts: body, soul, and spirit. And through these we look into a world of duality, seeing good and evil, light and darkness. Einstein saw something different. We are spirit moving at the speed of light that has slowed down to the thought of soul and hovers to manifest the body. In Genesis 1:2, the Spirit hovered over the face of the deep.

We are a lot deeper than we think. We have been singing a song for eons, and that song is now being heard as the Everlasting Gospel. God declaring, "Let there be light" was not an after effect of the Spirit hovering over our face in the deep—it was the same expression coming from a journey at the speed of light. Did He speak at that time, or was it a memory of a speaking before time that brought the sound to hover for expression to come forth?

Let us look at the structure of the atom to get more clarity. The atom can be broken down into three parts – protons, neutrons, and electrons. Each of these parts has an associated charge, with protons carrying a positive charge, electrons having a negative charge, and neutrons being neutral, possessing no net charge. In accordance with the Standard Model of particle physics, protons and neutrons make up the nucleus of the atom, while electrons orbit it in a "cloud".

In the Triune version of God (or the three-dimensional realm of God), we can see a connection. The positive protons represent the Father's perspective. When Jesus was baptized, there came a voice from Heaven, saying, "This is My Son in whom I am well pleased" (Matthew 3:17). Jesus had not yet entered the temptations in the wilderness to prove He was a worthy Son, so why affirm Him? Because the perfect man, Jesus, was not considered perfect by man's standard, but by the nature of the Father. It was the affirmation of the Father that postured Jesus to overcome in the first place.

The Father's perspective is what allows us to see ourselves as we truly are. Do I obey God to be approved by Him, or do I obey because I *am* approved? Obedience by faith and through grace is based upon the truth that we are already perfect in Christ, and this perfection is based in the Father's nature.

The negative electron is likened unto the Holy Spirit, who leads us into the unknown by the process of unveiling the truth. I do not want to put the Holy Spirit in a negative light, but the negative is really not bad. If you know anything about power, you need a negative wire to ground the positive power or it will overload the system (just like when you have to jumpstart your car battery). We want to run from all the things we deem negative in life, yet those are the seasons in which we are grounded and secured in our true identity.

Jesus was led by the Spirit into the wilderness of His mind. He had taken upon Himself the perception of man, and He had to untwist what ego was throwing at Him. Luke 4:1 tells us Jesus was filled with the Spirit before walking through the mind of man. In Luke 4:14, He returned in the power of the Spirit. As He shifted man's negativity through the Father's perspective, He brought the frequencies of thought into the divine; then Jesus could demonstrate what was believed.

The neutron is neutral, as Jesus only did what He saw the Father doing. Jesus knew who He was because He knew who His father was. In a finite mind, He funneled His memories from eternity into his human awareness. But He could only do this by bearing witness to truth. Bearing witness is observing without opinion or conclusion. There could be no judgment, no box to fit God in.

We get offended because of our conclusion-boxes that stem from a wrong perspective of the Father. When I cannot see the Father's motives concerning me, then I will distort my own image as a son. This will be seen in my reactions to try to control my life with reason, conclusion, and opinion. Our neutral posture of bearing witness to the truth in the midst of good and evil, positives and negatives is what decides which frequency we will inhabit. That frequency will determine the quality of our human life. All three parts of the atom are needed for life to prosper!

Electrons orbit as a cloud. And we are surrounded with a cloud of witnesses (Hebrews12:1). The unity of the faith is where we see the perfect man arise—manifesting the full stature of Christ is as the many, yet as One. While the electron is on the outer layer of the atom, it also lies at the heart of why we became human in the first place. It was unity that sent us, and it will be unity manifested at the end of the matter. As we discern the Father's perspective in the midst of opposites, we remember the reason we came. The love we all shared in Him before time began.

These three ingredients or layers of life also reveal a journey. Going deeper into a subatomic state, we can find what is called a "quark." A quark is any of a number of subatomic particles carrying a fractional electric charge, postulated as building blocks of the hadrons. Science is still unveiling the layers within the atom and how many quarks are inside. Quarks have not been directly observed, but theoretical predictions based on their existence have been confirmed experimentally. Break open this quark, and eventually you get to the center of light that is likened unto a circular vibrating string (1 John 1:7, John1:4,9).

Our spirit is neutral, and yet the two sides of the brain can be at odds, filled with both positive and negative thoughts. Once we realize every negative thought or ion grounds the positive, we will operate in unity at a human level, just as we do at a subatomic state.

You see, our atoms are all communicating with each other at the speed of light. We are at perfect harmony and unity as light. We cannot see an atom, but we see the human-sized results. Because atoms are not seen with the natural eye, this places them in the unseen realm or outside of time and space. Our human perspective has been limited, and it seems that the bigger we are in a physical reality, the slower we move and the more confused we become.

We as humans measure distance by inches, by feet, and by miles; therefore we also measure our life by time. But in the quantum realm, our lives are the sound of memory moving at the speed of light, like a wheel in the middle of a wheel. There is no beginning and no end. From this place, we measure dimensions from a multiverse, not by inches or feet.

The strongest telescope tells us the closest star is four light years away. What that actually means is that it was four light years *ago*. When we look at the stars, we are not seeing the present but the past; the past has yet to catch up to the present. There is no telescope in the world that can see an atom. We can only get an idea of atoms through powerful MRI machines that view through vibration.

Imagine the magnification required to see an atom! Are atoms really small, or are we simply trying to see them from time and space? In our three-dimensional awareness we would say that atoms are too small to see, but from eternity we see a magnified journey echoing from one dimension into another.

This is how deep we really are. There isn't one stranger among us at a subatomic state. The quantum realm has a visible and an invisible state that freely flow in and out with no limitations. This is the heart of eternity and the Everlasting Gospel: to remove the lies of a finite conclusion that has prevented us from seeing one another as one. In order for this to happen, we must see the positives in the midst of negatives so that we can stand neutrally, just as an atom does (Romans 8:18-22).

FAITH IS A HOUSEHOLD!

As we have therefore opportunity, let us do good unto all men, especially unto them who are of the household of faith (Galatians 6:10).

But having the same spirit of faith, according to what is written, "I BELIEVED; THEREFORE I SPOKE," we also believe; therefore we also speak (2 Corinthians 4:16).

Just as we have billions of cells at a subatomic level, we are a community. The many as one man! Particles are communicating without separation at the speed of light. Coming to the unity of the faith as a perfect man is realizing no one is separated. The lie of separation takes me out of a family and makes me an orphan. We are manifesting as light, sound, and form. This is what it means to go from glory to glory!

If we get entangled with the cares of this life, we are only conscious of form. But when we realize origin, we are as the stars that Abraham spoke to. We are also in the sound of the promise of God to Abraham having a son (seed of Christ). The sound, which is light slowed down, releases frequencies that manifest as forms or physical consciousness. This would be all the nations being blessed through believing Abraham.

Light slowed down to sound. Sound hovering brings expression or form.

Out of the throne proceeds rivers (Revelation22:1) and out of our bellies flow rivers (John.7:38). Spirit is fluid as a river in a third dimension, but it had another form before it looked like a river! It was waves of frequency coming into form through sound and light. Because we are in the faith, we are gathered together, and this is when the human experience appears. Just as in Genesis 1:9, waters gathered together to one place, so it was on the day of Pentecost when the believers were all of one mind and one accord in one place. There came a sound from Heaven as a wind as a suddenly! The natural coming from the movement and interaction of the spiritual. God said, "Let there be light." Jesus is the light, and the Word became flesh.

When Enoch encountered God, he did so at the speed of light. He witnessed it outside of time and he became invisible through translation. He moved at the speed of his encounter.

Elijah heard the sound of rain. He experienced a slowed-down version of what Enoch saw. Elijah was able to outrun the chariot by what he heard. Elijah's physical form moved at the speed of what he heard.

Faith comes by hearing. Have you heard Wisdom cry out? That is who you were echoing as a remembrance so that who you are as faith can arise within your human experience.

By faith Enoch was taken away so that he did not see death, "and was not found, because God had taken him"; for before he was taken he had this testimony, that he pleased God. But without faith it is impossible to please Him, for he who comes to God must believe that He is, and that He is a rewarder of those who diligently seek Him (Hebrews 11:5-6).

The posture of Enoch to translate or return to the original blueprint of existence has three keys:

1. Enoch did not rely upon natural understanding. Without faith it is impossible to please God. Enoch had to first realize origin as faith in order to operate from the place from which he was sent.

2. Enoch lived in the present embrace—
believing God *is*, right now! This requires a
revelation of what has been suffered in the
past in order to get the mind to live from the
present. Our minds live from where we have
been in our earthly journey. Where there are
conclusions outside of the Father's purpose,
then there will be the perception of loss and
lack. When we are stuck in the wrong
perception, we only react to the present from
the past. But the revelation of what has been
suffered enables the mind to be a witness of
the present without conclusions. A present
embrace is where I encounter God and am
aware of Him.

3. Enoch encountered an instant answer to
prayer, becoming what he had seen. Jesus
said, "Believe you have received, and you will
have it." Enoch became what he saw and
embraced it. He was transfigured! This is how
Jesus walked when He only did what He saw
the Father doing.

Quantum Glory

For the earth shall be filled with the knowledge of the glory of the LORD, as the waters cover the sea (Habakkuk 2:14).

Quantum glory is summed up as who we were in Him in the unseen realm, manifesting on Earth as we are in Heaven. By grace, through faith we are saved or awakened into our sonship in Christ. Since we are faith in the quantum realm, then the expression of us as faith is seen as glory in our human experience.

While faith is the substance of things hoped for, it is through grace that intention in the midst of demonstration is revealed. Grace in our human experience is really glory, or God's intentions. Who you were as faith is the substance of His intentions. Your humanity is the visible evidence of who you are as faith that reveals glory as grace. This is a divine reflection that needs to be realized as substance through spirit and evidence in our visible human experience.

Moses found favor, or grace with God. It was always there, and he realized it at the appointed time. He was awakened to the mystery hidden before the foundations of the world (Colossians 1:26-28). When God passed before Moses on the mountain, He put His hand over Moses in the cleft of the rock. He then removed His hand and allowed Moses to see the back side of Him. Moses was hidden in Christ the Rock; he saw what was finished or behind when he saw the backside of God. He saw the multi-membered body from the foundation of the world in that moment.

When Moses came down from the mount, his facing was shining with what he had seen (Exodus 33:17-23). Everything that God made that was good passed before Moses. It is the goodness of God that leads us to repentance (Romans 2:4). Moses was shining with the eternal singularity of Spirit—that which was good. His mind was changed and the veil of duality was removed.

Unfortunately, the Israelites still had a slave mindset because of their past perception in Egypt, so they wanted Moses to put a veil over his face because they feared true identity reflecting and confronting the mistaken identity they had settled for. But we see a parallel here with Jesus going up to the Mount of Transfiguration in Matthew 17:17. Jesus had just spoken to Peter about what He was about to suffer. Peter responded out of fear and ego. Jesus was going to need a different perspective, a higher frequency, in order to embody prophecy, so that's why His response to Peter seemed so harsh ("Get behind me, Satan ..."). On the mount, Jesus put on future glory by transfiguring. He tasted of the glory that would be revealed in the midst of what He was about to endure. We also see Moses and Elijah are present in this encounter.

I believe when Moses experienced the fullness of Christ in the cleft of the rock and seeing the finished work in the backside of God, there was a divine exchange. Jesus as a multi-membered body awakened divinity in Moses's human experience, knowing that what was remembered of divinity in Moses would be a deposit for Jesus's future human experience to remember Himself. Whatever Moses received in his generation, he took with him to the Mount of Transfiguration. So when Moses went up to the mount in his generation, where was he really going? To a future generation known as transfiguration. It was the future imparted to Moses and carried through generations within the DNA or sound of the blood. The Body of Christ has always held the memories of the mind of Christ.

I shared previously a little example of quantum entanglement. Let us review that with some added flavor. John 3:13 tells us, "And no man hath ascended up to heaven, but he that came down from heaven, even the Son of man which is in heaven."

On Earth as it is in Heaven is the reality of your identity in eternity walking in a parallel movement of both realms simultaneously. Just as quantum entanglement teaches that when two particles are entangled, no matter the distance between the two, they will move in tandem. as gears move counterclockwise to one another in a well-oiled machine, so who we were as faith moves and who we are as glory reflects. We are both particles! Our identity in eternity is Wisdom crying out to the simple (Proverbs 1:20). This is the Spirit of Wisdom and Revelation in the knowledge of Him!

The fellowship of suffering is the counterclockwise motion in our human counterpart. While we live in bliss and glory in eternity as spirit, we experience a finite distortion of sorrow and suffering in the timeline. The goal here is in the realization of being seated in heavenly places, or being heavenly minded, that begins to shift our reality. This convergence is known as the Kingdom suddenly upon you!

Once you live in the realization of this living epistle, you will view your entire life on Earth as it is in Heaven! You will not look for confirmations from God about what you think He wants you to do. Instead, you will see what was in Heaven, realizing it has already been done. Eternal confirmations can be seen as an overlap of a realization that *I have been here before and I have done this before*. It is confirmed to our human counterpart. Many of the revelatory encounters we receive are echoes of our identity trying to get the attention of our conscious human awareness.

Once awakened in the timeline, we will rise above it, standing on time. God's timing is everything, and it is not based on our earthly events, but upon heavenly reality.

Do you want to see God answer prayer quickly? How about prophecy fulfilled? Pray and prophesy outside of time! Hearing the original sound before time releasing you into time to become prophecy fulfilled.

For therein is the righteousness of God revealed from faith to faith: as it is written, the just shall live by faith (Romans 1:17).

That the God of our Lord Jesus Christ, the Father of glory, may give unto you the spirit of wisdom and revelation in the knowledge of him: The eyes of your understanding being enlightened; that ye may know what is the hope of his calling, and what the riches of the glory of his inheritance in the saints, And what is the exceeding greatness of his power to us-ward who believe, according to the working of his mighty power (Ephesians 1:17-19).

Let us break this down as a divine reflection or quantum echo. While faith in eternity is us as righteousness, we unveil this faith through glory, which is also known as grace in our human experience. Grace unlocks the Father's intentions in order to know and mirror the glory we had with Him before the world was. Within the glory, which is us, there are multiple interactions and reflections we will call layers of our identity, just as an atom has layers.

1. Before time you were Wisdom, and in time you are Revelation.

2. Knowledge is the conscious awareness of purpose that bridges these dimensions of glory.

3. The hope of His calling is to know the purpose for which we have been sent.

4. Riches, glory, and inheritance are what Wisdom used to build her house, which is the human experience (Proverbs 3:16-20).

5. The exceeding greatness of His power toward us who believe is the manifest glory that is emanating from the unseen journey into

the seen realm of time and space. (This is what is called quantum glory!)

At a quantum level in our human experience, we know we are moving at the speed of light, as strings of frequency connecting the dots and expanding into what we currently view as matter or form. While our human consciousness sees dimly the truth of our reality, our subconscious has eyes that see the memories of who we were before being born into humanity. This is known as a "sanctified imagination," or the reality of our origin. 1 Corinthians 13:12 tells us, "For now we see through a glass, darkly; but then face to face: now I know in part; but then shall I know even as also I am known."

To know as we are known, or have always been known by God, requires a mirror reflection in meeting ourselves in the future. This is known as prophecy! While prophecy is your face in the future human experience, you are prophecy sent forth. Your future here on

Planet Earth is your history in eternity looking at you from a present place of embrace. The testimony of Jesus is the Spirit of Prophecy, and you overcame by the word of your testimony before you ever came to Earth.

Now the Lord is that Spirit: and where the Spirit of the Lord is, there is liberty. But we all, with open face beholding as in a glass the glory of the Lord, are changed into the same image from glory to glory, even as by the Spirit of the Lord (2 Corinthians 3:17-18).

Going from glory to glory in a quantum world is ever before the face of the Father. The ongoing expression and face-to-face conversation outside of time is a race that has been run throughout the generations of time. In the same way that we search our thoughts before we speak in a conversation, so is the divine interaction to think a thought that is manifested as the generations of the heavens and the earth.

Chapter Eight

Manifested Sons of God

For the earnest expectation of the creature waiteth for the manifestation of the sons of God (Romans 8:19).

There has been a lot of shifting, shaking, and unveiling of truth overtaking the church in this season. For many generations there has been the proclamation of a time in which the sons of God would come forth and revolutionize Christianity as we have known it. I think many have expected this movement to fit into all the little boxes of what has been known. Many have left the church as it has been known because of the tug of war over holding fast to the traditions we have learned or letting the Spirit lead us into a new wineskin.

Reformation has never experienced an easy transition. It pulls the rug of what you have known right out from underneath you. We then want to question the validity of the truth currently being emphasized.

I want to encourage you in the stripping process that is now taking place. I myself struggled to let go of what I had known. To not be embittered with what was known as though I had been deceived the whole time; this is how many think. But if the truth I once knew is no longer valid, then how do I know what is presently being taught is truth?

We go from glory to glory in the unveiling of our identity. Being complete in Christ and going from glory to glory can be confusing. We are simply unveiling truth that we already had into a clearer picture of the Father's intentions. We couldn't see it before because the journey was the mechanism to unveil it.

For so an entrance shall be ministered unto you abundantly into the everlasting kingdom of our Lord and Savior Jesus Christ.

Wherefore I will not be negligent to put you always in remembrance of these things, though ye know them, and be established in the present truth. Yea, I think it meet, as long as I am in this tabernacle, to stir you up by putting you in remembrance (2 Peter 1:11-13).

Knowing the truth without making conclusions about it will enable you to enter present truth. Present truth is the living embrace of who God is in you and you in Him. It comes by being put in remembrance of these things. So you must use all previously known truths as steppingstones into the heart of the matter.

When I began this journey of living in the now from a neutral place, I had to let go of my need to understand by logic alone. Allowing the Lord to use what now appears to be obsolete as a bridge to others is very important. You're seeing the same truth, just from a different angle. We are graduating from the emphasis of doing into the reality of being.

The way we view revival will now change as the sons of God emerge. We will no longer try to get God to move for a revival, as though it is an outside source coming down upon a city. Instead, we will realize that in Him we live and move and have our being (Acts 17:28). We *are* revival! And when it seems quenched, it is because we are not being vulnerable and connected to the rest of the Body of Christ. The old-time revivals were about a man who had all the goods. Now it is about the Body of Christ being fitly framed together.

What about repentance? We have been taught that you need to confess your sins and that this is repentance. Without doing this. God cannot forgive you. Esau sought repentance with tears and never found it (Hebrews 12:17). But with the manifest sons of God, repentance means "to change your mind"--to realize you are not alienated from God and no longer an enemy because the separation and warfare were all in your mind. The wrong perceptions of our past has caused us to become enemies in our own minds (Colossians 1:21). Having godly sorrow because you did something wrong is perfectly normal. It is called having a conscience. This, however, is not repentance—but it leads to it.

We must first understand God's nature. Jesus healed the sick and forgave sins without any requirements (Matthew 9:5). He told multitudes who didn't even know Him that it was the Father's pleasure to give them the Kingdom (Luke 12:42). God has always looked like Jesus. And when we view God as legalistic in the Old Testament and a loving Father in the New Testament, then we struggle to find the balance in how we appropriate the scriptures.

1 Corinthians 13:5 tells us love keeps no record of wrongs. So how can God forgive me when He has never held anything against me? God is love, and when we accept forgiveness from Him, it is based on the reality that He has always accepted us. My mind changes in this reality, realizing I am accepted in the beloved.

This is how Jesus overcame as a man. He knew He was loved unconditionally by the Father.

My confession of sins is then redirected to forgiving myself. When I embrace the truth that I am fully pleasing to God, do I do this based on my works or His nature? Under the Law, God was an angry wrathful God, ready to smite me when I messed up. This is like the difference between a child who grows up in a healthy family and one who is abused. Which child will succeed in life?

Jesus came to reveal the balance and how you are to approach the Father. When I read the Old Testament, I no longer try to discern the nature of God through the eyes of those who saw Him from a place of self-condemnation. The Bible is a mirror of where you are in your journey of awakening.

All scripture is given by inspiration of God, and is profitable for doctrine, for reproof, for correction, for instruction in righteousness (2 Timothy 3:16).

The key here is defining what it means to be in righteousness. Walking like Jesus walked has nothing to do with self-effort or performance. His perfect sacrifice was not based upon obedience to the Law but upon the nature of the Father. He only did what was pleasing to the Father (John 8:29). What was pleasing to the Father? To only receive how the Father sees me. In this place my actions can now demonstrate obedience from a place of being fully loved.

All scripture is inspired, but what does this mean? It means that every possible perspective man had of God is hidden in every person whose stories have been recorded in the bible. And those perspectives are a mirror of where you are in the journey of unveiling identity. There are contradictions in the scriptures but this does not diminish God's purpose in using it.—This helps to adjust our perception of the nature of God.

The Bible corrects us by using every wrong perception of God to adjust what we have believed from a twisted view. Many take it upon themselves to correct one another when it comes to doctrines, but Christ is the only pure doctrine.

Let the Bible correct your intentions when you see Him as wrathful and angry. "But the Bible tells us God is like that," people say. No, it doesn't! It tells us *how we see Him*. It is the testimony of Jesus that is the Spirit of Prophecy. And when the Old Testament does not look like Jesus, then it is how man has reduced the image of God through the Tree of Mistaken Identity. Is the Bible still valid today? I believe it is. But there are two extreme narratives taking place right now that need to find balance.

One camp says, "I only believe what is in the Bible." I can agree with this if everything we see looks like Jesus and the Father—if when I gaze into the scriptures, I look into the perfect law of liberty and can bring unity through the truth. But if the truth you cling to divides the Body, then it is not the truth that sets you free.

The other camp says, "The bible is just a book that men wrote to manipulate us and control us." Yes, men wrote it. God has always spoken through people. We are made in the image of God. When we want to throw out the baby with the dirty bathwater, it is because we are still wounded from past religious experiences. Anyone can handle the Word of God deceitfully. When I have to defend what I believe at the expense of my brother, then I have yet to believe what I defend.

We as Christians tend to forget about fruit. What fruit is being produced? Relational fruit is what we are looking for, not doctrinal accuracy. Have you ever considered why Jesus did not order scribes to follow Him around and write down everything He said and did? Many think that He did do this, yet the dating of the scriptures say otherwise. We see Jesus writing in the sand but not writing a book. I believe He knew man's tendencies to return to slavery through indoctrination.

When I read the scriptures, I look through three lenses for the foundation on which I discern. First, I look through God as divine. He is all-knowing, all-powerful, and everywhere at once. Take this away and redemption has no power. Upon His divinity is the next lens, which is redemption as the finished works of God. And through these two lenses, I see and believe that God is love. From this place I search the scriptures to find my sonship in Him and the rest of the unified body of Christ. This is how we profit from the scriptures—the same way that Jesus did it. He searched Himself in the scriptures, and we are His body.

So how does the baptism of the Holy Spirit fit
into this eternal Gospel in which we were sent
with the Holy Spirit already in us?

The same way that Jesus exemplified this. God
became a man by the Holy Spirit. Jesus was
God and was filled with Himself (Holy Spirit)
while He was in the womb. He was then
baptized in the Jordan River, and the Spirit
descended again upon Him. When we realize
that Father, Son, and Holy Spirit are one God,
we will have to acknowledge that God came
upon Himself and within Himself in Christ.

On Earth as it is in Heaven is the posture for
remembrance. Our humanity will walk out
parables of the Kingdom that are not adding
one thing to who you have always been as
spirit. It is the mind that is awakening through
embodying on Earth what has always been in
Heaven.

In the first century, we see Jesus fulfilling
prophecy that was given to Israel. The feasts

were used as the outward manifestation for their minds to bear witness to the truth. God will meet us where we are when it comes to our ability to see. We see dimly, and then we see face to face. We will know as we have been fully known (1 Corinthians 13:12).

We get stuck in what God was doing and we make it the Gospel. But Hebrews 6:1-3 says:

Therefore leaving the principles of the doctrine of Christ, let us go on unto perfection; not laying again the foundation of repentance from dead works, and of faith toward God, of the doctrine of baptisms, and of laying on of hands, and of resurrection of the dead, and of eternal judgment. And this will we do, if God permit.

The way we implement repentance is by changing. The way we implement faith is by changing. When we change, all these doctrines will take on a new view.

Have you ever been standing at a distance and seen someone or something moving from far away? You just saw a form and couldn't tell if it was a person or an animal. But as you got closer, you could see more clearly. Maybe then you saw that it was a person. If you walked a little closer, you could tell whether it is a man or a woman. But you couldn't see the expression on the face of that person unless you came face to face with them.

This is what growing into maturity looks like—s seeing dimly but then face to face. Much of our Bible knowledge has been discerned from a distance. We concluded and built our doctrines. Then when someone came and showed us something we had never seen, we were suspicious. Our doctrines produced the fruit of suspicion.

This was how the Pharisees looked at Jesus. To them He was a heretic, and to many today the sons of God will look like heretics and false prophets.

We need to hold loosely what we believe and cling tightly to the One whom we have believed. Do not get too comfortable in what has been familiar. Treat your Bible study as an ongoing relationship. When we conclude the end of the matter, it is like concluding on a relationship—like coming to a period at the end of a sentence, when what we should be using is a comma. Once I believe I cannot know a person more than I know them right now, there will no longer be a relationship. But much like the comma tells us, the story must continue. It has not all been written yet.

Mystery inspires pursuit! The Father never meant for the scriptures to be agreed upon in the way we have sought agreement, which looks like attempting to make clones of people. We have too often defined unity as uniformity, and our "love" has extended only as far as our agreement. You are right and I am wrong? Look through the lenses of divinity, redemption, and love, and you will never go wrong. Realize that our diversity is what brings truth to life. Look from a different angle and you will see people as living epistles who are carrying your inheritance.

So how do we pray now from a place of already being complete? Since we no longer need to try to get something from God as though we are lacking we gaze into the fellowship of the Father and the Son. We commune, we embrace, and we watch Him move through us and to us. All the mechanical Christianity goes out the door and family flows together as the Father in us is doing the works.

And it shall come to pass, that before they call, I will answer; and while they are yet speaking, I will hear (Isaiah 65:24).

It is a mystery! Yet the Everlasting Gospel would tell us that from where you were called, you were sent as the answer to your generation. Being the answer to prayer is where we are going if God permits. Or shall I say, if we are willing to break our boxes. We will go from prophesying to becoming prophecy fulfilled in each others' lives. 1 Corinthians 13 tells us that when the perfect comes, then that which is in part will go away. This has nothing to do with the gifts of the Spirit being invalidated as though they are no longer needed. It is about only seeing part of the truth and then coming into the fullness of truth. And that fullness is love.

The gifts of the Spirit in 1 Corinthians 12 will also begin to unfold into a fuller revelation. Instead of the church competing against and comparing among themselves who is more gifted and anointed, we will realize we are gifts one to another. 1 Corinthians 12:12-13 says:

For as the body is one, and hath many members, and all the members of that one body, being many, are one body: so also is Christ. For by one Spirit are we all baptized into one body, whether we be Jews or

Gentiles, whether we be bond or free; and have been all made to drink into one Spirit.

The sons of God will emphasize equality within the Body of Christ. This is what it means to come into the unity of the faith, into a perfect man. We have walked through the generations of the sons of man, but now it is time to go unto maturity as sons of God. Our equality with the Father will produce security and true humility. This effect will be seen in the absence of striving and competition among the brethren.

Self-condemnation is what has enticed the church into indoctrination. Let me just say this: we all have a theology and there is nothing wrong with knowing what you believe. This is important. But what has *motivated* you to believe what you believe? Fear of loss? The need to protect yourself? Fear of deception? Fear of being a disappointment to God? When we build our beliefs to protect ourselves from intentions like these, then we will see the fruit of carnality in our midst.

Our best example is how Jesus walked and overcame. The way in which He postured Himself is foreign to twenty-first-century Christianity. We have built up our doctrines from a belief in the lie of lack. Hoping that all our spiritual warfare and intercession will somehow change the world has been the pursuit for a long time. Unfortunately, when we don't see the fruit we expected, we build another doctrine explaining why it didn't work. So how did Jesus do it?

Let us look at four different revelations that Jesus operated in that enabled Him to walk in the fullness of God.

The Father sent Me (John 20:21)

Jesus knew from whence He came and where He was going. He knew this before He ever overcame anything. He was secure in the Father because He knew His intentions. When we are blind to our purpose in our daily lives, we will struggle with insecurities and doubts.

When we think this way, we will look for knowledge to attain something or to deliver us from something. This is where we build our doctrines. Jesus, on the other hand ,believed that there was only one power—the Father. Therefore, Jesus did not have to understand what might have been hidden in His present situation because He knew it would present itself when it was time.

The Father is with Me (John 8:29).

Not only did the Father send Jesus on assignment, but He was always present every step of the way. We, in our human frailties, are always looking for confirmations and signs to see if God is with us. We judge outwardly in order to believe He is blessing us. This is because we really do not yet believe in the integrity of who the Father really is. We fend for ourselves because the Father might become disappointed with us if we fail Him. Yet, the opposite is true. Jesus knew He was fully complete in the Father. Jesus did not fear loss because He knew the Father had sent Him and would walk through everything with Him.

The lie of separation continues to speak to the carnally minded Christian. *If I was once separated, I could be separated again! So I must have a plan just in case the Father leaves me again.* But Jesus knew His origin and from whence He came. He knew that separation was a mindset, not a reality. Therefore the image of His Father was never questioned.

I only do what is pleasing to the Father (John 8:29).

Can you look into the mirror and say that? That you only do what is pleasing to the Father? Most would say no, because they have not yet understood what is pleasing to the Father. The real question here is: what did Jesus do that was pleasing? And in doing it, was it based on

the works of the Law or the hearing of faith?
Was it based on performance or was it based n
grace?

I believe that Jesus is the perfect example of
walking in grace. He was without sin, yet He
was made perfect through suffering (Hebrews
2:10). Jesus led the way into redefining sin as
well as perfection or maturity. 1 John 3:4-6 tells
us that transgressing the law is what brings sin,
and in Him is no sin. Where are you? Chosen
in Him before the foundation of the world
(Ephesians1:4). Now it goes on to say those
who sin have neither seen Him nor known Him,
and this can seem pretty confusing.

Let us go back and read the first three verses
of 1 John 3 to see this more clearly.

Behold, what manner of love the Father hath
bestowed upon us, that we should be called
the sons of God: therefore the world knoweth
us not, because it knew him not. Beloved, now
are we the sons of God, and it doth not yet

appear what we shall be: but we know that, when he shall appear, we shall be like him; for we shall see him as he is. And every man that hath this hope in him purifieth himself, even as he is pure (1 John 3:1-3).

Here we see love bestowed upon us as sons of God. No requirements are mentioned here— just unconditional love. Now it gives us a progression of how this unveils in our lives.

We can be called as sons by the Father who sees us as complete, and yet we might not yet know what this looks like. When I am blind to the reality of how my Daddy sees me, I will be worldly in my thinking and consciously will not know Him. But when I am awakened to the truth that I already am a son, then I will be just like Jesus. Knowing that He is the firstborn of (and from within) many allows me to fully receive who I am. It is this truth that purifies me as He is pure.

So as we piece this together, we realize that Jesus as a man was seen as perfect and complete because He was His Father's Son. His sinlessness was not the absence of weakness, but only believing the truth about His identity as a Son in the midst of human frailties. This is what was pleasing to the Father.

So every time you choose not to condemn yourself or evaluate yourself or try to prove yourself, and you look to see how the Father sees you, then you are only doing what pleases Him. All your outward actions stem from how we see ourselves. So instead of looking good on the outside and pushing down all the inferiority on the inside, we receive how the Father sees us. It will work its way out, and we will model Christ through us.

The Father does the works (John 14:10).

Everything flowed naturally through the life of Jesus. Nothing was forced to happen. He went with the flow of every resistance, knowing it was the Father's opportunity to reveal Himself. What happens when you do not know what the Father is doing? What do you do? When you cannot see the Father doing anything, then this is your cue to do nothing. Do not react or try to deliver yourself. Do not "name it and claim it" because insecurities are beginning to surface. Many times, we deliver ourselves right out of the revelation that the Father is faithful.

We are put in situations to expose all the facades of orphan hood so that we can realize we are sons. Look for what the Father is doing in you and in others. Read between the lines of confrontation and look for opportunities for God's grace and faithfulness to be seen. In the life of Jesus, we see this pattern. He would give a parable, and then life would present situations to make that parable plain speech.

The hardest thing for us to do is to not try to fix everything.

We define ourselves by what we do--and when we feel helpless, we feel purposeless. But real purpose is revealed once all these beliefs are removed through reliance upon the Father doing it. This does not mean we just sit physically by and do nothing; the point is God is targeting the thing that drives us to act. Many times the Lord will use the illusion of delay to surface what is really motivating you to obey. When we do not get an immediate answer from God, we start projecting the fear of loss. Most of our spiritual-warfare doctrines, as well as our intercession, has been built upon the fear of loss rather than on the love freely bestowed upon us.

The Everlasting Gospel of Christ is about sonship. It is the other side of what we were once taught. There are so many teachings about who God is and they are wonderful. But unless we know who *we are* in Him and as

Him, we will not experience living partnership to the fullest here on Planet Earth.

The sons of God will bring the revelation of origin, grace and unity. While the Gospel of Christ was about the man Jesus, the Everlasting Gospel is about His Body. The sons of God will move in tremendous power and glory. But it will not be a one-man show; it will be all humanity as one in Christ, whether they are awake or asleep.

The walls of religion will fall and many who rejected Christ before will fully embrace Him. Why? Because unconditional love will be the heart of this Gospel, and the church will again become the friend of sinners.

Acknowledgments

This book would not be a reality without my lovely wife Shauna and my two tender hearted sons, Ayden and Seth. They are the inspiration that has mirrored the affirmation of the Father in and through my life. Others I would like to acknowledge; Shakeira Adina, Crystal Conard, Jackie Myers, David King, Andrew Medina, Alec Martin, Matt and Jes Jones, and Victor Villagrana.

You all have walked with me, encouraging and challenging me to keep going. You cheered me on and pulled my identity to the surface. Our interactions and expressions together is the heart of this book.

There are many others, too many to name that are not directly mentioned here but you know who you are. Thank you for being the epistle of Christ in my life. You have helped me remember who I have always been in the Father.

Made in USA - North Chelmsford, MA
1325315_9781735260105
08.03.2022 0910